Ask for the Ancient Paths

DISCOVERING WHAT CHURCH
IS MEANT TO BE

By James Guirguis

ANCIENT FAITH
PUBLISHING

Bringing the Ancient Christian Faith to the Modern World

CHESTERTON, INDIANA

Published by:
Ancient Faith Publishing
A division of Ancient Faith Ministries
P.O. Box 748
Chesterton, IN 46304

Printed in the United States of America

ISBN: 978-1-936270-63-7

22 21 20 19   11 10 9 8 7 6 5 4 3

FOR ISABELLE, LYDIA,
AND JULIANA

CONTENTS

Acknowledgments

There are many people I would like to thank for their part in bringing this book to life. I would, however, be negligent if I did not begin by thanking my Lord and God and Savior Jesus Christ. His presence in my life is the source of every good thing.

I'm thankful to the V. Rev. David Smith and Nicholas Chapman for providing initial insight and direction as I started down this journey of writing my first book. I would also like to thank the V. Rev. Gregory Lazarus Murphy for reading through the entire first draft and providing many notes and corrections to the text. Thank you to Fr. Gregory also for his great encouragement through the entire process. The community of St. George, New Hartford, deserves a big thank-you for being a wonderful, peaceful, supportive family to me and my family. Thank you to Katherine Hyde for her strong eye for detail and perfection. Thanks also to John Maddex for generously agreeing to write the foreword.

Many thanks to the V. Rev. Nicholas Sorensen, who has provided me with fatherly support, wisdom, and guidance over the years. I would like to say thank you to all my beloved friends and family. There are too many of you to name, but you know that your presence in my life is second to none. A great big thank-you to my daughters, Isabelle, Lydia, and Juliana—your youthful imagination is inspirational. To my wife, Jennifer, thank you for your loving support, and above all, for your constant friendship.

Rev. James Guirguis
Bright Week 2013

Foreword

After Peter's confession that Jesus was "the Christ, the Son of the living God," Jesus said, "On this rock [that confession] I will build My church, and the gates of Hades shall not prevail against it" (Matt. 16:16, 18). That Church was not an "invisible church." It was a living, organic, physical reality with specific structure, doctrine, and practice. In *Ask for the Ancient Paths*, Fr. James Guirguis challenges us to explore our roots as Christians. We might be surprised at what we discover.

As a lifelong evangelical, I had always assumed the Church disintegrated in the first or second century, only to be revived at the Reformation. I was taught that Christianity took an evil turn after the early persecutions in the arenas and drifted further and further away from its original intent and ideal.

Still, I had many questions about that faithful group in those early years after Christ:

» Was it a house church?
» Was the worship extemporaneous?
» Was the order similar to Jewish forms of worship or did they abandon that altogether?

» Was it performance-driven with members using their singing and/or speaking skills similarly to the Sunday morning service in many churches today?

» Was God addressed informally or formally?

» What was the leadership structure? Elders? Pastors? Bishops? Popes?

» How did the doctrine and theology compare with mine as an evangelical?

Moving backward from my present assumptions a century at a time, I made some scary discoveries. Once I got past the most recent century or so, things started to get interesting. Doctrine, style, structure, all looked and felt considerably different from where I had planted my flag. Then it occurred to me that I was approaching this all wrong. I needed to start with the Church of the first century and move forward century by century if I was going to find out what changed and by whose authority.

I expected the track to grow cold after Emperor Constantine legalized Christianity in the fourth century. But the same Church with its early bishops and faithful teaching kept right on going and spread. The distance between the bishops and parishes of the West and the bishops and parishes of the East made communication difficult, and relationships got strained. That difficulty eventually led to a schism between the East and the West, which in turn ushered in some of the changes and abuses that led Martin Luther to fight against the excesses and scandals of the West. The Church in the East held its course from apostolic times even to the present day!

This discovery changed everything. The standard for what I believed and how I interpreted the Bible now had ancient roots, or as Jeremiah put it, "ancient paths" (Jer. 6:16 RSV). If what

I believed today was different from what this ancient Church taught and believed, guess who had changed.

As you read this book, ask yourself frequently and with an open mind, "Why is my belief and my church different from this early Church, and on what basis or authority?" Most likely you were taught what you currently believe by someone well intended and based on their interpretation of the Bible. However, this ancient Church also loves and reveres Holy Scripture and wouldn't dream of teaching anything contrary to it. It draws on the wisdom of its own Tradition, going back to the beginning to interpret the Bible as was intended by its inspired authors.

If you are struggling with finding a church or feel a nagging discomfort about your current church, I invite you to think seriously about what Fr. James Guirguis has written and begin your journey to the ancient Christian faith.

—John Maddex
CEO, Conciliar Media Ministries
Bright Thursday 2013

Introduction

"I have come that they may have life,
and that they may have *it* more abundantly."
(John 10:10)

This is one of my favorite verses in the Bible. I want what the Lord Jesus promises, an abundant life. Maybe that is what we're all searching for. Some of us might be looking for it without even knowing it!

Most of us spend our lives working hard to achieve goals and trying to fulfill our many aspirations. For some the goal is better physical health; for others it is financial stability. Some are looking for academic success, and still others are simply looking for "a good time" in one form or another. Whatever our goals may be, each of us will make literally millions of choices over the course of our life. Sometimes the decisions we make almost without thinking about them are in fact the most important ones of our lives. These are the decisions that help us or hinder us in reaching our goals. This is especially true in the way we live our Christian faith.

When the Lord Jesus talks about abundance, I don't believe He is speaking of wealth and worldly success. Our Lord was very poor, as we read in the Gospels, yet everywhere in the New Testament we are encouraged to have Jesus Christ as our role model and example. So this life of abundance must be based on something more than earthly wealth or material possessions. If we look at the life of Jesus Christ, we see that abundance in life is found through a deep relationship with God.

Have we made the goal of an abundant spiritual life a priority in our lives? Have we ever taken the time to ask whether the way we live as Christians and the churches we choose to attend are helping us to reach that goal?

According to some estimates, nearly forty-three percent of all Americans attend church services on a weekly basis. Think about that. If we assume an average church service takes about an hour on Sunday morning, we are talking about at least fifty-two hours of church services a year. For some it will likely be double or triple that amount if we include Wednesday and Sunday evening services. But the point here remains the same: many of us are spending huge chunks of our life in church.

While many of us spend vast amounts of time in church, the truth is that many Christians live unfulfilled. Many Christians live hollow lives and struggle to find joy, quite the opposite of the abundant life spoken of by the Lord Jesus. Sadly, some of these folks never even stop to reflect on their situation.

We pay close attention to the doctors who examine us and make sure they are competent and caring individuals. We do the same thing with mechanics and plumbers. We want to know they can get the job done properly. Yet it seems we have a double standard when it comes to what we do on Sunday morning and how that affects the rest of our lives.

Is church a magical cure for the blues? Will it give you perfect ecstasy at all times? Will it make you a perfect human and take away all imperfection? Probably not. What I am suggesting, however, is that participation in the body of Christ should give us some discernible fruit, some signs of abundant life. In Galatians, the apostle Paul writes about the fruit of the Holy Spirit: "But the fruit of the Spirit is love, joy, peace, longsuffering, kindness, goodness, faithfulness, gentleness, self-control" (Gal. 5:22–23).

By attending a church we are usually admitting that in some way we are interested in God or heaven, or perhaps in being better people. Have we examined the actual results of our church attendance? Are we growing closer to God? Are we becoming better human beings with better relationships? Are we any less dysfunctional? Are we people who show the fruit of the Spirit in our lives? We look for results in every other aspect of life; why not this one? Do we expect any results from our church life or from our relationship with the Lord Jesus, or do we simply go through the motions?

We rarely take account of our lives. We often fail to ask ourselves whether the beliefs and practices of our various churches or denominations are true and authentic to the teachings of the Bible. While theories abound in the worlds of science, economics, and sociology, there is no use in following theories in the religious life. We have to follow the Truth. That is certainly true when we attempt to know God or to live a life based on the teachings of Jesus Christ.

The task of getting to know God is not theoretical; it is actual. The task of growing in our life of faith, our relationship with Christ, is not based on opinion or on feelings that can change from day to day or minute to minute. Because it deals with God, our faith must be squarely centered on truth. God is not subject to our opinions or thoughts concerning Him. He is not an electable official or a professor we can critique at the end of a semester. Following God is a choice that is not to be entered into lightly.

Attending the right church matters because that is the only way to receive the actual teachings of Jesus Christ. The right church gives us what we need and not simply what we want to hear. Attending the right church matters because each of us is sick and needs a hospital. It matters because what we believe influences the way we act and relate to the world around us. Attending the right church matters because church is supposed to bring us into a relationship with God, the source of all love, life, and joy. If we know God, why do so many of us still feel lost or alone in the world? If we know God, why do our churches continue to reinvent themselves?

Simply put, if the decision to attend church is an important one, is it possible that what church we choose to attend is even more important? We usually take our time choosing a spouse because we understand the importance of that decision. We will hopefully be with him or her for the rest of our life. But the reality is that a church brings us, or ought to bring us, into a relationship with God—and we hope to spend much more than one lifetime in His presence!

During conversations with others concerning various churches, the question of which denomination or group is right or wrong, true or false, will inevitably come up. In all the conversations I have had, one thing has become abundantly clear to me. This subject has real, tangible effects and consequences for our lives. The simple premise here is that all churches are not created equal. We don't have a problem making that statement about a department store or type of car, but we do hesitate when it comes to making definite statements about the value or worth of a church. The church we choose to attend is much more important than the type of car we choose to drive or the stores where we choose to shop.

This book is an invitation to reimagine everything you think you know about that place called church. Maybe you've never spent much time in any church, or perhaps you've spent too much time in them. If you are bored, tired, uninspired, or drained by your current church (or by the last one you attended), maybe this book is written for you. If you feel as if you have the heart of a weary and thirsty traveler and you are looking for a cool drink of water, it might be time to stop looking. If you find yourself unaffected by church, it is time to be affected! If you find that you are still lost or drowning in the sea of life, this might be your chance to take hold of the life raft. If you find yourself a stranger to God and His Church, it is time to be reintroduced.

1

Reading the Bible:
My Way or the Right Way?

The citizens of the United States of America are privileged to live in a country where we are generally governed by a set of standards that is well laid out in a venerable document called the Constitution of the United States of America. In many ways it is the "Bible" of American government.

Whenever a law is legislated and voted upon in Congress, it is likely to have to answer one question before it is passed: "Is it constitutional?" We likewise as Christians ought to be looking at the Bible, and specifically the New Testament, as a way to make sure that we are in line with the foundational teachings of our faith. That sounds simple enough, but the reality is far more complex.

Centuries ago, beginning around 1517, a monk named Martin Luther had a conflict with the Roman Catholic Church. He saw many abuses of power and authority and even some unbiblical teaching and doctrine. Because of this, Luther publicly made his grievances known and attempted to set forth a new standard for Christians everywhere. Among his many ideas was one called *sola scriptura,* which means "the Scriptures alone." This doctrine, according to Luther, meant that the only valid authority for the life of a Christian was the Bible. It is interesting to note that no one had ever taught such a thing before the sixteenth century.

Now let's fast-forward nearly five hundred years to 2013. According to the *World Christian Encyclopedia,* there are nearly 38,000 denominations of Christianity. The question this raises is, "If there is one Bible and there was one Jesus of Nazareth, then why are there so many different churches?" After all, we are taught by the apostle Paul that "God is not *the author* of confusion but of peace" (1 Cor. 14:33). Is it possible that God is pleased with this? If God is not the author of confusion, then why are Christians so confused about so much?

THE CONSTITUTION OF OUR FAITH

"Then the Spirit said to Philip, 'Go near and overtake this chariot.' So Philip ran to him, and heard him reading the prophet Isaiah, and said, 'Do you understand what you are reading?' And he said, 'How can I, unless someone guides me?'" (Acts 8:29–31).

As we read in the quote above, it is quite easy to be confused. It's completely understandable. Think about some of the modern issues that churches argue about. One church meets on Sunday; others, such as Seventh Day Adventists, teach that this is wrong and focus on Saturdays instead. Another church teaches that women should remain silent, while some insist that women can be pastors. Some churches offer the Eucharist (Communion) on a weekly basis, and others hold it rather infrequently. Some churches have a hierarchy of leadership such as bishops, priests, and deacons, while others might simply have a preacher or pastor and a board of elders or deacons. Still others have no formal leadership at all.

Churches disagree about far more important issues as well, from the way we are saved to the way we should minister to the world around us. Just a brief look at a few types of churches reveals quite different understandings regarding both doctrine and practice. This should surprise us, because nearly all of them claim the Bible as their sole source of authority.

How do we wrap our minds around a problem that has plagued the Christian community for at least five hundred years? We go forward by looking to the past. We go back to the Constitution of the United States of America.

All the laws and statutes of the United States are expected to comply with the written witness of the Constitution, in much the same way all churches are expected to comply with the teachings of the Bible. But the fact is some laws have been made that were unconstitutional. When these laws were passed, they were officially on the books until someone disagreed with them and challenged their constitutionality. Of course, thinking they were unconstitutional wasn't enough to make it so. At this point, if the individual or group was fortunate enough, they would get a hearing before the Supreme Court. It is the job of the justices of the Supreme Court to make certain a law is indeed constitutional. If it is not, they have the power to reverse the law and render it null and void. What these justices do is to interpret the Constitution. This power of interpretation is considered authoritative.

In some cases, the Supreme Court will even try to determine what the original framework was for a certain constitutional clause or amendment. They try to understand the founding fathers' context, and they often attempt to be faithful to the original intent of the Constitution. Without their interpretation, the text of the Constitution, though powerful, might be misused and misunderstood.

The Bible, like any document, must be interpreted properly. That might seem obvious, but those 38,000 denominations didn't create themselves. They were born out of thousands of different interpretations regarding this one Bible that we should consider inspired by God. But it doesn't have to be this way. The Apostle Paul exhorts Timothy to "rightly [divide] the word of truth" (2 Tim. 2:15). This verse has implications. There is a proper or "right" way to divide or discern the word of truth. Like the Ethiopian eunuch in Acts, we may also need someone to guide us.

The founding fathers of the United States had a firm idea about the Constitution—after all, they wrote it. They loved this country and used the Constitution as a guide for the generations that would follow after them. They understood a judicial branch of the government would have the proper power to interpret the Constitution when others had failed to do so.

So just like the nine Supreme Court justices, we must begin to ask the question, "What did the founding fathers mean?" Just as these justices try to determine what the original practice of the government might have been and what the original interpretation of the Constitution looked like, so we must also begin to look at the practices of the early Christians.

Of course the metaphor of how we interpret the Constitution, like all metaphors, is limited. However, the point remains the same. In order to shed light on the proper understanding of the Bible, we can't rely on a Christian Supreme Court. We also can't simply imagine the Bible is fully self-revealing. It may reveal some things clearly, but others are in need of clarification. We have to be brave enough to cross uncharted waters. We have to be ready to use all the resources at our disposal in order to form a better picture of how the early Christians understood the Bible and how they worshiped before the New Testament ever existed. This means we also have to be willing to look at sources besides the Bible.

AIDS TO INTERPRETATION

We've all been taught the Bible is the Word of God and that "all Scripture *is* given by inspiration of God, and *is* profitable for doctrine, for reproof, for correction, for instruction in righteousness" (2 Tim. 3:16). But how will that benefit us if thousands of denominations each read it according to their own whims and opinions and not according to God's truth? Let's get serious and think about what the Bible actually means instead of simply thinking about what the Bible means to me personally.

The Bible is profitable if we read it with the proper interpretation. When the Scriptures are used improperly, they become the opposite of profitable. They might even lead us away from the fullness of Christ. It is important to note that the passage above never states that the Bible is the sole, exclusive source for doctrine, reproof, correction, or instruction. God gave us minds, and there is no doubt He expects us to search for answers. As mentioned above in Acts 8, the Ethiopian eunuch had the Scriptures and was still lost. He needed an interpreter.

We have to be ready to use sources besides the Bible because everyone has an interpretation of the biblical text, and most of those interpretations differ. Nearly all the Jews living at the time of Jesus' earthly ministry read the Scriptures; many even knew them by heart. Yet we find that most of the Jews did not actually understand them. As the Lord taught them, "You search the Scriptures, for in them you think you have eternal life; and these are they which testify of Me" (John 5:39). Somewhere along the line, the Jews had missed something critical. Is it possible we also have missed a few things?

Think about it: Every Protestant church claims the Bible as its sole source of authority, and each church reads basically the same Bible. Yet we are left with the modern dilemma of having just as many readings of the Bible as there are denominations! The use of extrabiblical sources is important because it gives us an idea, a road map to the understanding and practice of the earliest Christians. This is even more important when we remember that early in the life of the Church, there was no New Testament in existence—just a few scattered books that would later become parts of the New Testament.

If we refuse to look at extrabiblical sources, we are saying we are comfortable in our own denominational interpretation of the Bible as the truth. But if you have a Baptist reading and I have a Roman Catholic reading, which reading is correct? There is one God-breathed Bible given to all in order to unite and not to divide. We know this because "no prophecy of scripture is of any private interpretation" (2 Pet. 1:20), and "God is not the author of confusion" (1 Cor. 14:3).

SEARCHING FOR FINE PEARLS

"Again, the kingdom of heaven is like a merchant seeking beautiful pearls, who, when he had found one pearl of great price, went and sold all that he had and bought it" (Matt. 13:45-46).

We have to follow the words of the Lord Jesus and become treasure hunters in search of fine pearls. To do that, we have to be ready to use whatever is at our disposal, including the historical record. History is taught to children from an early age in order to inform them of the foundations of our society, our culture, our country, and our collective struggles and victories. Christianity also has a history. It is not simply some faceless, thousand-paged book. Since the Christian movement is a historical fact that is attested to in multiple sources throughout history, it is to our benefit to search this record and be familiar with it.

One of the best ways for us to understand what we call "the mind" of the early Church is to take a look at some of the teachings of the early leaders of the Christian Church and see whether their ideas of church and our ideas of church can be reconciled. If we imagine the childhood game of "telephone," we are quick to admit that the closer we are to the source of the message (the Apostles in this case), the more likely we are to receive the whole message as it was meant for us.

It's not such a leap to trust the words of writers outside the Bible. From Martin Luther to John Calvin to John Wesley to Billy Graham to Rick Warren to your current pastor, you already trust certain people and consider some of them to be authoritative. The earliest Christians also considered some leaders to be authoritative. Many of these leaders lived a thousand or more years ago. They were godly men who were in complete communion with the one unbroken original Church that is found in the Book of Acts. This unbroken original Church still exists, and continues to consider some of these men to be authoritative voices. These figures are our link to the proper understanding of the Bible and the truths it holds. If the Bible is the map, they should rightly be considered the key.

After all, Christianity had a beginning. It didn't just appear out of nowhere in the sixteenth century with Martin Luther. It was not simply a corrupt Roman Catholic Church until that time. The Holy Spirit was working well before Luther was born. He has been guiding the Church for two thousand years. There is more to the story, but no one cared to share it.

The science fiction movie *The Matrix* includes a powerful scene in which a leader named Morpheus offers the reluctant hero-to-be Neo a choice. Listen to his words:

> *You take the blue pill and the story ends. You wake up in your bed and believe whatever you want to believe. You take the red pill and you stay in Wonderland, and I show you how deep the rabbit hole goes. Remember—all I am offering is the truth, nothing more.*

It is your turn now. You can close this book and remain comfortable in your current understanding of Christianity. You can imagine you know all there is to know about the Church. But there is another option. This is your red pill—the truth about the Church and all the things Jesus meant for you to have and to share with Him.

The choice is yours. Are you ready?

2

The Church That Existed Before the New Testament

"The past is always a rebuke to the present."
—Robert Penn Warren

We often hear that the only source of authority in the life of a Christian is the Bible, and specifically the New Testament. Now, please don't get me wrong—I love the New Testament. This small collection of twenty-seven books has changed my life more than any other book I have ever come across. But what about the first Christians?

Well, the problem is that they didn't have a New Testament to turn to for help. Imagine living as a Christian without the aid of the epistles of Paul or the Gospels. In fact the first books of the New Testament, the letters of Paul, were not written until twenty or thirty years after the Crucifixion of Jesus. Also keep in mind that most people were illiterate and could not read those books once they were written. To make matters even more complicated, the New Testament as a complete work was not compiled and accepted by the Church until roughly AD 367. In that year it was a letter from Athanasius, Archbishop of Alexandria, Egypt, that officially named all the books of the New Testament, while rejecting many that were not considered authentic or instructive for the salvation and life of a Christian.

Are we expected to believe that the earliest Christians simply holed themselves up in caves and waited until the books of the New Testament were written decades later? If that had been the case, there would be no Christianity at all. It would have become extinct. Fortunately for all of us, that did not happen.

If we briefly look at a few verses from the New Testament, we will see clues to help us understand how the early Christians got along without the Bible.

"But we command you, brethren, in the name of our Lord Jesus Christ, that you withdraw from every brother who walks disorderly and not according to the tradition which he received from us" (2 Thess. 3:6).

Please notice here that the apostle Paul does not refer the faithful people of Thessalonica to the New Testament. Only a few of his letters existed at this time. Instead we see that Paul refers them to "the tradition" that was "received from us." Unlike written sources of instruction, *tradition* refers to what is passed down orally or by word of mouth.

Many Protestants have been taught that tradition is a Roman Catholic invention. But the Apostle Paul speaks about it a number of times, and we know he wasn't Roman Catholic. Here is another example: "Therefore, brethren, stand fast and hold the traditions which you were taught, whether by word or our epistle" (2 Thess. 2:15). Here we see that Paul appeals to the traditions taught by the apostles, regardless of whether those traditions are put down on paper or given by word of mouth.

It is possible that this is all part of a Roman Catholic conspiracy. It is more likely, however, that we have somehow glossed over those verses. Sadly, it is probably true that some are familiar with them but have tried to imagine them away. It is possible that some Christians found the idea of tradition so problematic that they simply ignored it, or worse yet, had it demonized.

Such a thought is really shocking when you consider that every Christian denomination has traditions that are not fully specified or laid out in the New Testament. From the way we worship to our rules of order and local constitutions, we are sure to find plenty that is lacking in biblical reference. Altar calls and contemporary worship services are just a couple of examples that come to mind.

Hopefully by now we understand that it is possible that some of the teachings of the Apostles were never written down but were simply passed on orally to the faithful, and especially to the leaders of the early Church, as you will see.

The Church existed before the New Testament. It could not be any simpler than that. Try as we might to wiggle around that fact, we will still be faced with that first wall in our way to a better understanding of Christianity. The earliest Christians didn't look to the New Testament to answer their questions; most of them couldn't even read! They looked to their Church and its leaders. As it is written, "And they continued steadfastly in the apostles' doctrine and fellowship" (Acts 2:42). Both of these were key ingredients to being a Christian. One had to believe the Apostles' doctrine, and one had to be in fellowship with them.

There's really only one conclusion to be drawn from this: The Church itself was an authority for Christians. Listen to the words of the apostle Paul: "But if I am delayed, *I write* so that you may know how you ought to conduct yourself in the house of God, which is the church of the living God, the pillar and ground of the truth" (1 Tim. 3:15).

Clearly Paul writes about the Church and calls it the house of God, but he goes even further, calling it "the pillar and ground of the truth." Just as important as what is written here is what is unwritten. Paul does not refer to the Scriptures or the New Testament as the pillar and ground of truth, or even to one particular apostle, such as Peter or himself. He refers emphatically to the Church as this powerful authority in the lives of Christians everywhere. Have we ever thought of the Church in this way?

If the Apostle Paul is referring to the Church, which one is he referring to? This is where things get interesting. Christian history as taught in most denominations is simply the story of how Christianity was saved from the corrupt Roman Catholic Church by Martin Luther and a few other notable names, such as John Calvin, John Wesley, Zwingli, and even Jan Hus.

I once spoke to a colleague who had attended a well-known Southern Baptist seminary, and I asked him specifically about his introductory course in Christian history. What he shared with me was shocking. He told me they spent the first semester going through the Christian timeline from the Acts of the Apostles to the Protestant Reformation. If you are keeping count, that is roughly one century of history a week for sixteen weeks. In contrast, my own experience in graduate studies took us through roughly four centuries in the same sixteen-week period. Either we went four times more slowly or they went four times more quickly! My gut reaction was that these folks had simply glossed over too much for such a course to be taken seriously.

While it is true that the Roman Catholic Church is an important part of Christian history, it is even more important to remember that Christianity existed in many parts of the world, not just Rome. As an illegal religion, the Church grew rapidly for the first few centuries after the Crucifixion and Resurrection of the Lord. This happened even throughout intense periods of persecution under certain Roman emperors. Under the protection of the Emperor Constantine, the Church began to flourish.

Large gatherings of the Christian bishops (ecumenical councils) were held at various times. Such councils dealt with serious doctrinal or theological controversies that were causing confusion in the churches. This brings us to an important event: the Great Schism.

The year 1054 is commonly regarded as the date of the event we call the Great Schism. This refers to the first major split of the Christian Church. Until this point in time, there was only one Church. Think about that for a moment. For nearly the first thousand years of Christianity, there was only one group of Christians in all the world. However, in the second half of the second thousand years of Christianity (from 1517 until the present), we have thousands more!

At the time of this schism, there were five great centers of Christianity: Alexandria, Antioch, Jerusalem, Constantinople, and Rome. Each of these was led by an archbishop or patriarch who was in full communion and fellowship with all the others.

Because of a great dispute among the five, there was a break in communion. A split occurred, and four of the archbishops along with the Church in the East continued on one path, while the Christians of Rome under the leadership of their archbishop (called the pope) separated from the rest.

Now we know what happened to that church in Rome. It became the Roman Catholic Church, the one that is often referred to simply as the Catholic Church. But what about the other four centers (commonly called patriarchates)? What happened to them? Did they vanish or go extinct? No. They never vanished at all. They continued to exist for century after century, and they still exist now. Collectively they are known as the Orthodox Church.

Some people are familiar with the Russian Orthodox Church or the Greek Orthodox Church, but they are merely two of the largest national expressions of the worldwide Orthodox Church. There is so much more to the Orthodox Church than mere ethnicity. The Orthodox Church is the Church that has existed since the Apostles first preached the gospel of Jesus Christ. In fact, the Orthodox make the bold claim that they have not changed their beliefs or doctrine at all since apostolic times. For nearly two thousand years their faith has not changed. This has serious repercussions for all who call themselves Christians today.

If what the Orthodox Church claims is indeed true, we all have quite a bit to learn about the Christian faith. We will spend the next few chapters surveying the beliefs of the Orthodox Church, their scriptural references, as well as a few quotes from leaders of the early Church regarding each of these beliefs. Remember that everyone quotes the Bible, and many do so improperly. So we might benefit from being able to hear the thoughts of well-known leaders of the early Church, in much the same way that we might study the writings of the founding fathers of the United States for insights into how they saw the world around them and how they understood their role.

Now let's make a deal. Any time you are ready to close the book and decide that it doesn't agree with your denomination, whether that be Lutheran, Southern Baptist, charismatic, Pentecostal, Episcopalian, evangelical, or otherwise, I'd like you to take the "roots test." Ask yourself, "When did my church begin? What are its roots?" If the roots don't clearly lead back to the apostolic community that existed even before the New Testament was written, then how can you be sure that such a community is living up to its potential? How can you be sure that it is interpreting the Bible properly and is well pleasing to God?

Our church or denomination may mean well, and we may be surrounded by a great group of people who love Jesus, but meaning well was never enough according to the Lord Jesus Christ. In John 4, the Lord Jesus encounters the woman at the well, a Samaritan (a non-Jew). This woman compares the way the Jews worship to the way the Samaritans worship, and then she is faced with reality according to Jesus Christ:

> *You worship what you do not know; we know what we worship, for salvation is of the Jews. But the hour is coming, and now is, when the true worshipers will worship the Father in spirit and truth; for the Father is seeking such to worship Him. God is Spirit, and those who worship Him must worship in spirit and truth. (John 4:22–24)*

Most of the churches mentioned have the right spirit, and certainly they have a portion of the truth. But taking a closer look at the early Church and, by extension, the Orthodox Church will give us an idea of how some denominations have gone wrong or may simply be lacking.

We love Jesus Christ, and we want to grow in Him and feel His presence growing in our lives. We also love His Church, which is both His Body and His Bride. I want to have everything He meant for me to have and not simply someone's misunderstanding or misreading of it all. God wants to give us an extravagant feast rather than cold leftovers!

The following chapters will highlight a few of the areas that make the Orthodox Church unique. Each area we will cover has tremendous potential to change the way we view God and relate to Him, and that has the power to change our lives.

Remember taking the red pill? Now it is time to see just how deep the rabbit hole goes.

3

How Faith Works

For a long time, many churches have focused on defining how we are "saved" as Christians. The argument as it has been described by many is one of faith versus works. Before we tackle this issue, we need to remember that doctrines don't simply exist in books or in some neat bubble by themselves. They attach themselves to our lives and become a part of us. What we believe dictates what possibilities are available to us in life and even what actions we will take or fail to take.

As an extreme example, let's look at one of the doctrines of the Jehovah's Witnesses. This group has the belief that we should never receive blood transfusions for any reason whatsoever. In fact it is forbidden, based on their misreading of the biblical teaching against ingesting blood. This belief, of course, would have major implications in the life of an individual who suffered from a serious trauma or injury with the loss of blood. In the event of an accident, what a Jehovah's Witness believes could lead to an unnecessary death that could easily have been prevented through a transfusion. Clearly, what we believe dictates what possibilities are available to us and what choices we will make.

This brings us back to the issue at hand. We are looking at the argument of the role of faith versus works in our eternal salvation. Martin Luther (the same man who gave us *sola scriptura*) also pushed Christians to believe firmly in *sola fide* (faith alone). As we dig deeply into this subject, let's remember that Luther lived in the sixteenth century. By that time Christian doctrine was already quite well established throughout Christendom.

Now nearly all Protestant denominations or churches believe that we as Christians are saved from the wrath of God by faith or belief in Christ. They use verses such as these to defend such a claim:

"For God so loved the world that He gave His only begotten Son, that whoever believes in Him should not perish but have everlasting life" (John 3:16).

"And he brought them out and said, 'Sirs, what must I do to be saved?' So they said, 'Believe on the Lord Jesus Christ, and you will be saved, you and your household'" (Acts 16:30–31).

"But now the righteousness of God apart from the law is revealed . . . even the righteousness of God, through faith in Jesus Christ, to all and on all who believe. For there is no difference; for all have sinned and fall short of the glory of God, being justified freely by His grace through the redemption that is in Christ Jesus" (Rom. 3:21–24).

"For by grace you have been saved through faith, and that not of yourselves; *it is* the gift of God, not of works, lest anyone should boast" (Eph. 2:8–9).

Orthodox Christians also believe in each of these wonderful verses. For Orthodox Christians, however, there is more to the matter; these verses present only half the truth. It is true that we are saved by the grace of God, but that doesn't necessarily mean what we would like it to mean.

An example of this was given to me by a mentor many years ago. Imagine you are walking down the street and you happen to bump into a wealthy banker (I'm picturing the Monopoly guy). As you are passing the banker, he decides to strike up a conversation with you, and in his benevolence he writes you a check for one million dollars. The banker also suggests you should quickly get to a bank and make a deposit. Now that you are holding a check in your hands, can you consider yourself a millionaire? Think about it: Are you holding a million dollars in your hands? No. What you are holding is a promissory note. The note has no value until you believe it is genuine and take action. If you simply left it in your pocket, it would be worthless. You must first believe that the check is real. You might say you have to have faith in the value of the check. Next you must get that check to the bank. Grace freely brought you the check without any work on your part and without your being worthy in any way. But grace will not force you to believe or walk you to the bank. The truth is that some work is necessary on your part.

The Christian life is a process of synergy, or cooperation, according to the Orthodox Church. We can only speak about cooperating with God because of His grace toward us. He loves us so much that He sent His only Son to us, and He did so freely! There was nothing we could do to gain God's favor. The Lord Jesus didn't take flesh and become a human because we were cute or lovable or good. Paul writes, "But God demonstrates His own love toward us, in that while we were still sinners, Christ died for us" (Romans 5:8). God's grace is shown to be true because God freely gives the gift of His Son, and that is the beginning of our salvation. The Lord shows His grace by choosing to suffer and die upon a cross with no strings attached. This grace is given to each and every man, woman, and child, regardless of who they are or what they have done in life, because Jesus Christ is "the living God, who is *the* Savior of all men, especially of those who believe" (1 Tim. 4:10b). Christ freely gives salvation to all, and it is up to each of us to enter into it. The Lord writes the check, and now we have to make a decision. The decision is whether or not we will accept it.

Many Protestants equate this decision with being "born again." They ask others when they were saved based on when they "made a decision for Christ." If we are familiar with Protestant churches, we will notice many of their services include an invitation to the front or an altar call designed to be a time to publicly proclaim Jesus as one's personal Lord and Savior. Many of these altar calls are emotional in nature. People who respond believe God will save them through this response. They will then boldly ask others if they "know for sure that they are going to heaven." Some Christians even believe that no matter what they do for the rest of their lives, they will be saved or enter into heaven based on this one momentary decision. Sadly for many, this is the closest they will ever get to knowing the Lord. For some the journey starts and ends there, with very little sign of true, meaningful change.

For the Orthodox, accepting the check or believing that it actually has value is similar to accepting the promise of salvation through Jesus Christ—it is just the beginning. Knowing that Jesus Christ is the Savior of the world, the long-awaited Jewish Messiah, is but a step. It is similar to a man picking out a ring and proposing to a woman he loves. If he spent the rest of his life simply being engaged and never working toward marriage, I assure you he wouldn't stay engaged for long! If you are hungry for a relationship with Christ, it might be time to read the rest of the relationship manual. Here is what it (the Bible) has to say:

"When the Son of Man comes in His glory, and all the holy angels with Him, then He will sit on the throne of His glory. All the nations will be gathered before Him, and He will separate them one from another, as a shepherd divides his *sheep from the goats. And He will set the sheep on His right hand, but the goats on the left. Then the King will say to those on His right hand, 'Come, you blessed of My Father, inherit the kingdom prepared for you from the foundation of the world: for I was hungry and you gave Me food; I was thirsty and you gave Me drink; I was a stranger and you took Me in; I was naked and you clothed Me; I was sick and you visited Me; I was in prison and you came to Me.'"* (Matt. 25:31–36)

"Then He will also say to those on the left hand, 'Depart from Me, you cursed, into the everlasting fire prepared for the devil and his angels: for I was hungry and you gave Me no food; I was thirsty and you gave Me no drink; I was a stranger and you did not take Me in, naked and you did not clothe Me, sick and in prison and you did not visit Me.' . . . And these will go away into everlasting punishment, but the righteous into eternal life." (Matt. 25:41–43, 46)

We see from the Lord's parable of the Last Judgment that He can't tell a lie. He cannot declare someone righteous based on a whim, or simply because we call Him Lord. We must be shown to be righteous as He Himself is righteous. Just in case this isn't clear, we can look at another verse also: "Not everyone who says to Me, 'Lord, Lord,' shall enter the kingdom of heaven, but he who does the will of My Father in heaven" (Matt. 7:21).

It is so clear as to remove any doubt whatsoever. The Lord reminds us in case we have any misconception about how things work. Even those who call Him "Lord, Lord," who in fact recognize Him and make this confession of faith, are not spared. The only one who is safe is the one who "does the will of my Father." As if that wasn't enough, look at this passage: "Thus also faith by itself, if it does not have works, is dead. But someone will say, 'You have faith, and I have works.' Show me your faith without your works, and I will show you my faith by my works. You believe that there is one God. You do well. Even the demons believe—and tremble!" (James 2:17–19). Martin Luther declared the whole epistle of James to be an "epistle of straw" because it so clearly contradicted his incorrect teachings. What a haphazard treatment of the Word of God!

We believe in one God, and that is great! Even the demons believe and are nearly scared to death. They not only believe in God, but in Jesus Christ His Son, as we see in the Gospel accounts of exorcisms. Yet those demons are fallen beings and far from salvation because they do not have love and do not do the things of God. John writes, "And the world is passing away, and the lust of it; but he who does the will of God abides forever" (1 John 2:17). It is the *doing* of the will of God that allows us to partake of God, who is Himself eternal and ever-existing.

Paul writing to the Christians at Galatia has a reminder for them:

Now the works of the flesh are evident, which are: adultery, fornication, uncleanness, lewdness, idolatry, sorcery, hatred, contentions, jealousies, outbursts of wrath, selfish ambitions, dissensions, heresies, envy, murders, drunkenness, revelries, and the like; of which I tell you beforehand, just as I also told you in time past, that those who practice such things will not inherit the kingdom of God. (Gal. 5:19–21)

We can call ourselves Christians until we are blue in the face, but that is not enough, according to the Scriptures. Paul was clearly reminding the Galatian Christians of their duties and obligation to act according to the Spirit and not according to the flesh, since it is the Spirit who gives life. As Paul writes elsewhere, "Therefore, my beloved, as you have always obeyed, not as in my presence only, but now much more in my absence, work out your own salvation with fear and trembling" (Phil. 2:12). Working out our own salvation with fear and trembling: that is what it means to be an Orthodox Christian.

The apostle Peter writes in his general epistle, "receiving the end of your faith—the salvation of your souls" (1 Pet. 1:9). If we believe that initial faith in Christ is the salvation of our souls, we don't understand the timeline. According to the apostle Peter, salvation is the end of our walk of faith, not the beginning.

According to the Orthodox Church, salvation is not simply about checking off some box in order to guarantee ourselves salvation. It is all about a relationship with God and His Son and Spirit:

"If you love Me, keep My commandments." . . . Judas (not Iscariot) said to Him, "Lord, how is it that You will manifest Yourself to us, and not to the world?" Jesus answered and said to him, "If anyone loves Me, he will keep My word;

and My Father will love him, and We will come to him and make Our home with him." (John 14:15, 22–23)

If obedience to Christ's commandments causes the Father to love us, it follows that the opposite is also true. If obedience gives us love, disobedience brings God's wrath. If following Christ allows Him to "make a home" with us, negligence leaves us empty.

It may be that some wanted to distance themselves from certain forms of Catholicism that infer a kind of works righteousness. It may also be that others simply misinterpreted the Bible. It could even be true that people dislike hard work. After all, we are a fast-paced, fast-food society, and we love quick and easy results, a sort of fast-food faith. Why would anyone want to work for something that is free, like salvation?

One thing is for certain: the possibility of growing in Jesus Christ vanishes when we don't live our faith. In fact that is one of the most interesting things about the words *faith* and *belief*—they don't simply refer to a thought in your head. They are both understood in the original Greek language of the New Testament to be life-changing convictions. If you are living in the same way as you did before you came to a belief in Christ, then according to the Orthodox you still have not believed fully in Christ, because He hasn't changed or redeemed your life. Faith is like a fire—it is dynamic and energizing to our whole life. There has never been a fire that didn't leave a sign of its presence. The same is true of a relationship with the Lord, because "He will baptize you with . . . fire" (Luke 3:16).

If I give up my million-dollar check or get tired and stop walking to the bank, then what will happen? In Hebrews we read, "For we have become partakers of Christ if we hold the beginning of our confidence steadfast to the end" (Hebrews 3:14). Our goal is Christ, and that goal is met when we "hold the beginning of our confidence [our faith] steadfast" until the end. The apostle Paul echoes this same idea when he writes, "*There is* therefore now no condemnation to those who are in Christ Jesus, who do not walk according to the flesh, but according to the Spirit" (Rom. 8:1). There is no condemnation for those who are in Christ, and those who are in Christ are clearly known by whether or not they walk according to the Spirit.

If at any point in time we lapse and fall away from Christ, we are falling away from the source of our life, our hope, and our salvation—and that is never a good thing.

Following are a few thoughts of early Christians leaders concerning the topic of faith versus works and how it relates to our salvation.

Ignatius, bishop of Antioch, led the church of Antioch from AD 68 until his death by martyrdom around 107. He was known to be a disciple of John the Apostle, and this has astonishing implications for us. The relationship of Ignatius to John tells us the Apostles left others in charge of the Church before they died. This means there was no need for Christians to try to interpret the New Testament blindly (the New Testament wouldn't be compiled for another couple hundred years anyway). Ignatius is also one of the earliest Christian writers outside of the New Testament, and he tells us much about the structure and practices of the early Church, as we will see later. Let's hear his words:

> *Seeing then that all things have an end, there is set before us life, based upon our observance of God's precepts, but death as the result of disobedience. And every one*

*according to the choice he makes, shall go to his own place.
Let us flee from death, and make the choice of life. (Letter to
the Magnesians, ch. 5)*

Athanasius, Archbishop of Alexandria (298–373):

*For by these things is the promise of eternal life, as Paul
wrote to Timothy, calling constant meditation exercise, and
saying, "Exercise thyself unto godliness; for bodily exercise
profits little; but godliness is profitable for all things, since
it has the promise of the present life, and of that which is
eternal." (Festal letter 11)[1]*

John Chrysostom, Archbishop of Constantinople (347–407):

*"He that believes in the Son has everlasting life" [John 3:36]
. . . "Is it enough, then, to believe in the Son," someone will
say, "in order to have everlasting life?" By no means! Listen
to Christ declare this Himself when He says, "Not everyone
who says to Me, 'Lord! Lord!' shall enter into the kingdom of
heaven" [Matt 7:21]; and the blasphemy against the Spirit
is alone sufficient to cast him into hell. But why should I
speak of a part of our teaching? For if a man believes rightly
in the Father and in the Son and in the Holy Spirit, but
does not live rightly, his faith will avail him nothing toward
salvation. (Homilies on John, 31:1)*

*"If salvation is by grace [Rom 11:6]," someone will say,
"why is it we are not all saved?" Because you did not will
it; for grace, even though it be grace, saves the willing, not
those who are unwilling and who turn away from it and*

who constantly fight against it and oppose themselves to it.
(Homilies on Romans, 18:5)

We've shown here that there is more than one way to read the Bible and that the early reading of the Scriptures regarding faith and works is quite different from the reading proposed by Martin Luther and other Reformers. When we misread the Bible, we make a liar of God, and we lead people down the wrong paths by giving them a false sense of hope and a cheap sense of the value of salvation. We are assuring them they are saved even while their actions show them to be slaves of the flesh and of the world, which are passing away. In fact we are reminded that calling Christ "Lord" means we are called to be slaves to Him and to no other person or thing.

True Christian faith works, and it strives diligently to avoid worldly temptations and to stay the course. Works are the proof that we have believed in Jesus Christ in a way that is more than simply intellectual or emotional. Works are proof that we have a firm and life-changing conviction. It is good to remember that what we are speaking about here is not some form of works righteousness; it is a form of faith that is fully alive and shown to be true in practice. Works can't save us; it is works that demonstrate that we are indeed saved people with the fingerprint of God all over our lives.

4

Biblical Leadership

We as twentieth-century American Christians have some very peculiar ideas about leadership. This is probably a direct result of living in a land that was founded and based on religious freedom and individual rights. We each seek to be our own master in life, and this is all the more true when it comes to religion. While we may love democracy as a political force, we sometimes need to be reminded that democracy was not the way of the early Christians or of the Scriptures. In seeking to find what is missing in our church life, we must address the topic of church leadership. We aren't interested in what feels good; we are interested in worshiping and praying in the way the early Christians learned from the Apostles, who learned from the Lord Himself.

We all know what happens when we set out to complete a project and everyone wants to be the leader or chief: chaos ensues! Everything breaks down rather quickly. As the saying goes, "There are too many chiefs and not enough Indians." What is clear throughout the Scriptures is that no man ever takes on the authority of leading the people of God without being chosen by God. Individualism will get us nowhere. The truth is that certain men had the charism of leadership, and this gift was not chosen by the individual but given by God in a systematic way. God in His wisdom delegated the task of building up His Church in a particular way. Let's start by taking a look at some of the biblical references to leadership, and afterward let's see how the early Christians understood the subject.

We are told in Luke 6:13 that the Lord Jesus chose twelve from among His many disciples to be His chief apostles. According to Luke 10:1, the Lord also chose seventy men to be apostles, and He sent them out in pairs. So these men led the ministry of the Church early on. We see that after the Resurrection of our Lord they were given a special gift to do so: "And when He had said this, He breathed on *them,* and said to them, 'Receive the Holy Spirit. If you forgive the sins of any, they are forgiven them; if you retain the *sins* of any, they are retained'" (John 20:22–23).

As the number of the faithful increased, the Apostles decided to pray for deacons to help with the table service (distribution of food and alms to the needy):

"Therefore, brethren, seek out from among you seven men of good reputation, full of the Holy Spirit and wisdom, whom we may appoint over this business; but we will give ourselves continually to prayer and to the ministry of the word." And the saying pleased the whole multitude. And they chose Stephen, a man full of faith and the Holy Spirit, and Philip, Prochorus, Nicanor, Timon, Parmenas, and Nicolas, a proselyte from Antioch, whom they set before the

apostles; and when they had prayed, they laid hands on them. (Acts 6:3–6)

It is important to note that the seven men who were chosen for this ministry received the laying on of hands from the apostles in much the same way the apostles received the Holy Spirit from the Lord Jesus in the passage from John 20. In each case there was a clear and lawful transfer of power, if you will. What is utterly absent throughout the Scriptures is the idea of a self-appointed leader.

Even in the case of Paul, we see that although he was called by the Lord Jesus Himself, he was told to go through the proper channels by first visiting Ananias:

Now there was a certain disciple at Damascus named Ananias; and to him the Lord said in a vision, "Ananias." And he said, "Here I am, Lord." So the Lord said to him, "Arise and go to the street called Straight, and inquire at the house of Judas for one *called Saul of Tarsus, for behold, he is praying. And in a vision he has seen a man named Ananias coming in and putting* his *hand on him, so that he might receive his sight." Then Ananias answered, "Lord, I have heard from many about this man, how much harm he has done to Your saints in Jerusalem. And here he has authority from the chief priests to bind all who call on Your name." But the Lord said to him, "Go, for he is a chosen vessel of Mine to bear My name before Gentiles, kings, and the children of Israel. For I will show him how many things he must suffer for My name's sake." And Ananias went his way and entered the house; and laying his hands on him he said, "Brother Saul, the Lord Jesus, who appeared to you on the road as you came, has sent me that you may receive your sight and be filled with the Holy Spirit." (Acts 9:10–17)*

After this we see that Paul spent time with the Apostles:

But Barnabas took him and brought him *to the apostles. And he declared to them how he had seen the Lord on the road, and that He had spoken to him, and how he had preached boldly at Damascus in the name of Jesus. So he was with them at Jerusalem, coming in and going out. (Acts 9:27–28)*

In Acts 15 we have the story of the Jerusalem council. "Therefore, when Paul and Barnabas had no small dissension and dispute with them, they determined that Paul and Barnabas and certain others of them should go up to Jerusalem, to the apostles and elders, about this question. . . . Now the apostles and elders came together to consider this matter" (Acts 15:2, 6). Here we see the importance of unity and oneness of mind for the Apostles. Even when there was a dispute, they came together and prayed and reasoned for the proper response without anyone acting individually. Paul and Barnabas did not follow the modern approach of breaking communion and starting their own denomination or group based on their own understanding. They sought the approval and wisdom of those who had been rightly appointed as leaders. By actions such as these, they showed themselves to be truly filled with the Holy Spirit and guided by humility and the love of Christ. Christian leaders continued to meet in such councils throughout the early life of the Church.

In the early Church, besides the rank of apostle, there was a clerical hierarchy consisting of bishops, presbyters, and deacons.

How does this fit in with the priesthood of all the faithful?

The Orthodox Church believes that all Christians are priests. St. Peter teaches, "But you *are* a chosen generation, a royal priesthood, a holy nation, His own special people" (1 Pet. 2:9). This certainly means that each of us is a priest because the Lord Jesus is our High Priest, as seen in the Epistle to the Hebrews, and each one of us is meant to be "priestly"—that is, to pray on behalf of the whole world.

But this is not the end of the story. We also see that in the New Testament there was a sacramental priesthood. This group was charged with the task of leading the Christian communities and administering the sacraments (*mysterion* in Greek). As Paul wrote, "Let a man so consider us, as servants of Christ and stewards of the mysteries of God" (1 Cor. 4:1). So in fact we see the apostle telling us that he is a steward of the mysteries or sacraments. This group of sacramental priests acts as priests to the priests. They minister to those who minister to the rest of the world.

We see the example and foreshadowing of church leadership, unity, and order already evident in the Old Testament. "Then Nadab and Abihu, the sons of Aaron, each took his censer and put fire in it, put incense on it, and offered profane fire before the LORD, which He had not commanded them. So fire went out from the LORD and devoured them, and they died before the LORD" (Lev. 10:1–2).

Can we begin to imagine the seriousness of the matter? If the Lord treated the sons of His lawful priest this way, imagine how all those who are unlawfully acting as presbyters, elders, and shepherds might be seen through the eyes of God? An even better example of this is found in the story of the rebellion of Korah.

Now Korah the son of Izhar, the son of Kohath, the son of Levi, with Dathan and Abiram the sons of Eliab, and On the son of Peleth, sons of Reuben, took men; *and they rose up before Moses with some of the children of Israel, two hundred and fifty leaders of the congregation, representatives of the congregation, men of renown. They gathered together against Moses and Aaron, and said to them, "You* take *too much upon yourselves, for all the congregation* is *holy, every one of them, and the* Lord *is among them. Why then do you exalt yourselves above the assembly of the* Lord*?" . . .*

Then Moses said to Korah, "Hear now, you sons of Levi: Is it *a small thing to you that the God of Israel has separated you from the congregation of Israel, to bring you near to Himself, to do the work of the tabernacle of the* Lord*, and to stand before the congregation to serve them; and that He has brought you near to* Himself, *you and all your brethren, the sons of Levi, with you? And are you seeking the priesthood also? Therefore you and all your company* are *gathered together against the* Lord*" (Num. 16:1–3, 8-11a).*

So the Lord *spoke to Moses, saying, "Speak to the congregation, saying, 'Get away from the tents of Korah, Dathan, and Abiram.'" . . . And the earth opened its mouth and swallowed them up, with their households and all the men with Korah, with all* their *goods. So they and all those with them went down alive into the pit; the earth closed over them, and they perished from among the assembly. (Num. 16:23–24, 32–33).*

At this point some might be thinking that these examples are all from the Old Testament, and that is certainly true. But it is important to remember that we believe the God of the Old Testament is the same God of the New Testament. We also believe that God does not change, since "God *is* not a man, that He should lie, / Nor a son of man, that He should repent" (Num. 23:19). God always took the priesthood seriously, and while the order of the priesthood changed from the priesthood of the Temple to the priesthood of Christ, it was not abolished (see Heb. 4:14—5:10). God is the God of details, precision, and order, especially when it comes to ministering the mysteries of the Kingdom to His holy flock. Jesus Christ was and is our high priest. He never abolished priesthood anywhere in His teachings, but instead revealed its true nature through His ministry and sacrifice.

In the New Testament, we see that Paul instructed Timothy to appoint (ordain) presbyters and deacons in every place. We see the same thing happening in Acts: "So when they had appointed elders in every church, and prayed with fasting, they commended them to the Lord in whom they had believed" (Acts 14:23). Now this word *elder* is important because it comes from the Greek word *presbyteros* and should in fact be translated as *presbyter*, another word for *priest*. The *Oxford Dictionary of the Christian Church* explains the word *presbyter* in this way: "The English word 'priest' derives ultimately from this root (*presbyteros*)" (p. 1119).

Regarding the position of bishop, the *Oxford Dictionary* says, "The highest order of ministers in the Christian Church. The word Bishop is an Anglo-Saxon corruption of *episcopus* (overseer)" (p. 176).

There is some possibility that the words *bishop* and *presbyter* may have been used in the New Testament interchangeably to a degree, but this seems to be a simplistic understanding, based on all the evidence. For example, all bishops are also presbyters, and in fact we even see that the apostle John refers to himself as "the presbyter" (see 2 John 1:1). Even in modern times, a man who is made bishop must first be ordained as a presbyter. It should also be noted that while all bishops are presbyters, not all presbyters are bishops. Perhaps a modern equivalent would be found in the way we might call various people working within a church "ministers," including the pastor. But we would never call the various other ministers "pastor."

It also seems likely that because of the small size of the Christian communities at the time the New Testament was written, there was probably little need for more than a bishop in most areas. Since a bishop functioned as a priest, he would be the *de facto* presbyter of the community. When the community grew too large for one bishop alone, he would then ordain other presbyters to assist with the ministry in one geographic territory under his guidance.

The role of the bishop is to oversee a group of church communities. He acts as a sort of district manager. He is a living symbol of unity and a prayerful leader for the people and clergy under his jurisdiction. He can also administer all the sacramental mysteries, including the ordination of presbyters and deacons.

Presbyters are typically leaders of a single local church community. They are pastors who teach, preach, and can administer all the sacramental mysteries with the exception of ordaining other presbyters or deacons.

Like bishops and presbyters, deacons have had various roles throughout history. In Acts we see them tasked with the function of serving tables and distributing to the needs of the poor. In modern times they function to assist presbyters and bishops with many of the day-to-day pastoral responsibilities, including prayer and worship services as well as the sacramental mysteries.

Since we've looked briefly at the New Testament references to church leadership, let's see what the voices from the early Church taught.

Ignatius, Bishop of Antioch, wrote:

For as many as are of God and of Jesus Christ are also with the bishop. And as many as shall, in the exercise of repentance, return into the unity of the Church, these, too, shall belong to God, that they may live according to Jesus Christ. Do not err, my brethren. If any man follows him that makes a schism in the Church, he shall not inherit the kingdom of God. (Epistle to the Philadelphians, ch. 3)

It is therefore befitting that you should in every way glorify Jesus Christ, who has glorified you, that by a unanimous obedience you may be perfectly joined together in the same mind, and in the same judgment, and may all speak the same thing concerning the same thing [1 Cor. 1:10], and that, being subject to the bishop and the presbytery, you may in all respects be sanctified. (Epistle to the Ephesians, ch. 2)

For if the prayer of one or two possesses such power, how much more that of the bishop and the whole Church! He, therefore, that does not assemble with the Church, has even by this manifested his pride, and condemned himself. For it is written, God resists the proud. Let us be careful, then, not to set ourselves in opposition to the bishop, in order that we may be subject to God. (Epistle to the Ephesians, ch. 5)

As therefore the Lord did nothing without the Father, being united to Him, neither by Himself nor by the Apostles, so neither do anything without the bishop and presbyters. (Epistle to the Magnesians, ch. 7)

See that you all follow the bishop, even as Jesus Christ does the Father, and the presbytery as you would the Apostles; and reverence the deacons, as being the institution of God. Let no man do anything connected with the Church without the bishop. (Epistle to the Smyrnaeans, ch. 8)

It is not lawful without the bishop either to baptize or to celebrate a love-feast; but whatsoever he shall approve of, that is also pleasing to God, so that everything that is done may be secure and valid. (Epistle to the Smyrnaeans, ch. 8)

While it may seem like Ignatius is being harsh, we should take notice of his tone. He is serious about the government of the Church. Repeatedly we see him teaching all of these churches the proper way to maintain order and unity in the Church of God. And who can blame him, "for God is not *the author* of confusion but of peace, as in all the churches of the saints" (1 Cor. 14:33).

If this is the teaching of one of the first bishops of the Christian church, a disciple of John the Apostle who was well regarded and universally admired, then who are we to reimagine doctrines to fit our own liking or our own understanding? If we see that our church life is a confusing mess or we feel lost, perhaps we are lacking bishops and priests to guide us.

It is important to remember that anyone can call himself a bishop, much as anyone can call himself a cat. Just because someone takes that title for himself doesn't make it so. In their wisdom, the early Church had a few ways of recognizing true bishops from those who were false. Irenaeus, Bishop of Lyons in France, writing in the second century, has this to say:

> *It is within the power of all, therefore, in every Church,* who may wish to see the truth, to contemplate clearly the tradition of the Apostles manifested throughout the whole world; and we are in a position to reckon up those who were by the Apostles instituted bishops in the Churches, and [to demonstrate] the succession of these men to our own times. (Against Heresies 3.3.1)*

> *And this is most abundant proof that there is one and the same (life-giving) faith, which has been preserved in the Church from the Apostles until now, and handed down in truth. (Against Heresies 3.3.3)*

What Irenaeus is speaking about is a phenomenon known as apostolic succession. It is the idea that those who are true teachers and bishops of the Christian Church must have been appointed by those who were themselves the Apostles of the Lord Jesus or their direct disciples. This safeguard, which is still present to this day, prevented any rogue individuals from taking the title of bishop for themselves and teaching whatever they

---

* The use of the word *Church* here refers to various locations and not to denominations.

felt like teaching. These men were all accounted for and known to be true teachers of the faith who were ordained by those who were already trusted leaders of the Church.

A positive example of this is found in Acts:

It seemed good to us, being assembled with one accord, to send chosen men to you with our beloved Barnabas and Paul, men who have risked their lives for the name of our Lord Jesus Christ. We have therefore sent Judas and Silas, who will also report the same things by word of mouth. (Acts 15:25–27)

We also see an example of the opposite:

Then some of the itinerant Jewish exorcists took it upon themselves to call the name of the Lord Jesus over those who had evil spirits, saying, "We exorcise you by the Jesus whom Paul preaches." Also there were seven sons of Sceva, a Jewish chief priest, who did so. And the evil spirit answered and said, "Jesus I know, and Paul I know; but who are you?" Then the man in whom the evil spirit was leaped on them, overpowered them, and prevailed against them, so that they fled out of that house naked and wounded. (Acts 19:13–16)

What if one of those bishops broke rank with the others? What if they taught the wrong things? It was possible then, just as it is now, for some who call themselves Christian leaders to teach false doctrines. Even Paul has this in mind when he tells his disciple Timothy, "Hold fast the pattern of sound words which you have heard from me, in faith and love which are in Christ Jesus" (2 Tim. 1:13).

There was a pattern of sound teaching, and this was to be

maintained at all times or punishment was to be applied. The most potent form of punishment was to break communion with (excommunicate) those who held false teachings. The Lord Jesus taught, "And if he refuses to hear them, tell it to the church. But if he refuses even to hear the church, let him be to you like a heathen and a tax collector. Assuredly, I say to you, whatever you bind on earth will be bound in heaven, and whatever you loose on earth will be loosed in heaven" (Matt.18:17–18).

The Apostle Paul also writes, "Now I urge you, brethren, note those who cause divisions and offenses, contrary to the doctrine which you learned, and avoid them. For those who are such do not serve our Lord Jesus Christ, but their own belly, and by smooth words and flattering speech deceive the hearts of the simple" (Rom. 16:17–18). We should remind ourselves of how many divisions already exist among Christians and just how serious these divisions are in the eyes of the Lord Jesus.

Yet another safeguard against rogue, independent bishops was the use of church laws or canons regarding the proper ordination or consecration of a new bishop. The thirteenth canon of the council of Carthage (AD 394) states, "A bishop should not be ordained except by many bishops, but if there should be necessity he may be ordained by three."[2] This again was a clear safeguard set in place to prevent one rogue bishop going out and ordaining other bishops on his own authority. In the Orthodox Church, a level of cooperation and unity is expected among all leaders, especially the bishops of the Church.

We've taken a brief look at the way in which church leadership and structure was understood from ancient times up until the present time. It is worth noting that the only church or denomination that has continued with this unchanged teaching regarding the role of bishops, priests, and deacons is the Orthodox Church.

It is a historical and biblical fact that some were appointed apostles, bishops, priests, and deacons. In fact we can go so far as to say that without the leadership of bishops or presbyters within our churches, we are not following the Bible. Far from simply trusting ourselves and leaning on our own understanding, each member of the Church is invited to look for guidance and leadership from one of these God-ordained men.

Finding the Church that has men who are rightfully appointed to these roles puts us in a position to receive guidance from those who are experienced in the Way. Finding the right Church puts us in the position to receive the mysteries of God from men who are stewards of those mysteries. Finding the proper hierarchy of Christian leadership gives us an opportunity to receive the many blessings God has to offer.

5

A Mysterious Life

One of the major differences between the Orthodox Church and the various denominations in existence today is the belief in the sacraments or holy mysteries (*mysterion* in Greek). The apostle Paul writes, "Let a man so consider us, as servants of Christ and stewards of the mysteries of God" (1 Cor. 4:1). The Orthodox Church teaches that there are seven major sacramental mysteries, and they are as follows: priesthood or holy orders (which we covered briefly), Eucharist (Holy Communion), baptism, chrismation, confession, marriage, and unction of the sick. In contrast, most Protestant groups believe in only two sacraments: communion and baptism. They tend to view these as merely symbolic, having no supernatural effect, and call them "ordinances." They are often referred to as outward signs of inward changes, having no power in and of themselves.

The Orthodox belief in the mysteries is founded on the belief that the Lord Jesus, the only begotten Son of God, really took flesh and became man like one of us. He lived in space and time and interacted with the world around Him. Because of His interaction with the world, especially through His Crucifixion, the whole world is transformed and takes on a new character and new meaning. As Paul writes, "He might gather together in one all things in Christ, both which are in heaven and which are on earth—in Him" (Eph. 1:10).

In addition to acknowledging what the Lord has done by becoming man and living in our world, we have to honor what He Himself taught concerning these sacramental activities. For the Orthodox, the mysteries are a fundamental way in which God interacts with His people. If we simply reduce "being a Christian" to believing the right thing about Jesus, then we have missed the point of the Christian life. Christianity is not another philosophical system. The point of the Christian life is not simply to believe the right thing but to enter into life with Christ, to commune with Him and feel His presence grow in our lives. As Peter writes, "that . . . you may be partakers of the divine nature" (2 Peter 1:4).

In addition, the Orthodox Church is understood as a spiritual hospital, since each and every one of us is a sinner. We see sin as a symptom of the deeper underlying illness we all suffer, which is the rupture of communion with God. This division between God and man was caused by our rejection of Him and His commandments, as seen in the Garden of Eden.

Just as a hospital is useless without medicine, so is a church without sacraments. If we wonder why we are burned out or unaffected by church and why we still feel empty after all those years of listening to the preacher, singing the hymns, and following the praise and worship band, we should ask ourselves, How am I becoming a partaker of the divine nature, and how am I growing in spiritual health?

Wishful thinking isn't a solution to the problem. Seeking a relationship with Christ "living in our hearts" or feeling that we are "in the Spirit" during worship are abstract goals. Orthodoxy teaches them as concrete realities through the sacramental mysteries.

We will take a look at exactly what the New Testament teaches regarding these life-giving mysteries, and then we will see how the early followers of Jesus Christ understood this reality. Please keep in mind that each section is not intended to be exhaustive, but simply a brief introduction.

6

A Life of Communion

The subject of Holy Communion is one that is often debated in various Christian circles. People argue passionately about its meaning and purpose in their lives. Let's take a look at some of the references to this subject in the New Testament.

And as they were eating, Jesus took bread, blessed and broke it, and gave it to the disciples and said, "Take, eat; this is My body." Then He took the cup, and gave thanks, and gave it to them, saying, "Drink from it, all of you. For this is My blood of the new covenant, which is shed for many for the remission of sins." (Matt. 26:26–28)

And He took bread, gave thanks and broke it, and gave it to them, saying, "This is My body which is given for you; do this in remembrance of Me." Likewise He also took the cup

*after supper, saying, "This cup is the new covenant in My
blood, which is shed for you." (Luke 22:19–20)*

*For I received from the Lord that which I also delivered
to you: that the Lord Jesus on the same night in which He
was betrayed took bread; and when He had given thanks,
He broke it and said, "Take, eat; this is My body which is
broken for you; do this in remembrance of Me." In the same
manner He also took the cup after supper, saying, "This
cup is the new covenant in My blood. This do, as often as
you drink it, in remembrance of Me." For as often as you
eat this bread and drink this cup, you proclaim the Lord's
death till He comes." (1 Cor. 11:23–26)*

It is worth noting that in every one of these passages the facts
are the same. The Lord says, "Take, eat My body" and "Take,
drink My blood." Contrary to popular Protestant doctrine, there
is not one reference to a symbol anywhere in the words of the
Lord. So why are so many putting words in His mouth?

We Orthodox believe the bread and wine in Holy Communion
become the actual body and blood of the Lord. But that doesn't
mean we're cannibals. Part of the idea of a sacrament is that it
is mysterious. We don't know exactly how it works, because it is
a work of God, and God has revealed only certain things to us
in His wisdom. While some might feel less than satisfied with
that explanation, the Orthodox are quite comfortable with the
mystery of the unknown, because God is not fully knowable.
What we do know is that the bread and wine always look and
taste like bread and wine. The change is a spiritual one, and
spiritual changes, while invisible, are very real, as the Lord

Himself says: "It is the Spirit who gives life; the flesh profits nothing" (John 6:63a).

Do you wonder whether Jesus really meant His words literally? Consider this passage from John:

> The Jews therefore quarreled among themselves, saying, "How can this Man give us His flesh to eat?" Then Jesus said to them, "Most assuredly, I say to you, unless you eat the flesh of the Son of Man and drink His blood, you have no life in you. Whoever eats My flesh and drinks My blood has eternal life, and I will raise him up at the last day. For My flesh is food indeed, and My blood is drink indeed. He who eats My flesh and drinks My blood abides in Me, and I in him. As the living Father sent Me, and I live because of the Father, so he who feeds on Me will live because of Me. This is the bread which came down from heaven—not as your fathers ate the manna, and are dead. He who eats this bread will live forever. (John 6:52–58).

From the passage above it is clear that the Lord Jesus was really serious about this teaching and even equated it with causing life. The Lord also reminds those who are listening that when we eat of His flesh and drink His blood, we abide in Him and He abides in us. The Orthodox believe this to be true in a very literal way. It is true that many people have misunderstood the teachings of Christ and led us to thousands of divisions of the Church, but consider this: If the body and blood can give life, according to the Lord, we would also expect that they could pass on sickness and death if we did not take them seriously. In 1 Corinthians we see this is exactly the case:

Therefore whoever eats this bread or drinks this cup of the Lord in an unworthy manner will be guilty of the body and blood of the Lord. But let a man examine himself, and so let him eat of the bread and drink of the cup. For he who eats and drinks in an unworthy manner eats and drinks judgment to himself, not discerning the Lord's body. For this reason many are weak and sick among you, and many sleep. (1 Cor. 11:27–30)

So the body and blood of Christ can give either life or death, according to the New Testament. How many symbols do you know of that have the power to kill someone?

Finally, we have a wonderful passage in Luke:

Now it came to pass, as He sat at the table with them, that He took bread, blessed and broke it, and gave it to them. Then their eyes were opened and they knew Him; and He vanished from their sight. And they said to one another, "Did not our heart burn within us while He talked with us on the road, and while He opened the Scriptures to us?" So they rose up that very hour and returned to Jerusalem, and found the eleven and those who were with them gathered together, saying, "The Lord is risen indeed, and has appeared to Simon!" And they told about the things that had happened on the road, and how He was known to them in the breaking of bread. (Luke 24:30–35)

This passage is quite clear and to the point for those "who have ears to hear." The presence of the Lord is not even necessary because He truly dwells in the bread that He has just blessed and broken. That is why He vanishes from their sight. If this is not clear on its own, we are told these men went to the Eleven and told them "how He was made known to them in the breaking of the bread." This is not simply a matter of knowing the Lord because of the fact that He was the one who broke the bread. The men do not say that they recognized Him *when* He broke the bread, rather that they recognized Him *in* the breaking of the bread.

Instead of simply disregarding the interpretations that might not be convenient for us, maybe it is time for us to think about the repercussions these matters might have for our lives. The Lord Jesus wants to live and dwell within us in a literal and spiritual way. He wants us to be the temple where He lives. What a wonderful way of living! Is it any wonder so many of us feel hungry? We've been deprived of the Bread of Life.

Let's take a moment to look at the early writings of the Church regarding this subject. The earliest evidence for the proper understanding of the Eucharist outside of the New Testament is found in at least three distinct documents: the Didache; the writings of Ignatius, Bishop of Antioch; and the writings of Justin the Martyr. Let's allow them to speak for themselves as voices from the past.

The Didache, also known as the Teaching of the Twelve, was written between 80 and 120 and was even considered part of canonical Scripture by some church figures. Here are some excerpts:

> *Now concerning the Eucharist, give thanks this way. First, concerning the cup: We thank You, our Father, for the holy vine of David Your servant, which You made known to us through Jesus Your Servant; to You be the glory for ever.*
>
> *And concerning the broken bread: We thank You, our Father, for the life and knowledge which You made known*

to us through Jesus Your Servant; to You be the glory for ever. Even as this broken bread was scattered over the hills, and was gathered together and became one, so let Your Church be gathered together from the ends of the earth into Your kingdom; for Yours is the glory and the power through Jesus Christ for ever. . . .

But let no one eat or drink of your Eucharist, unless they have been baptized into the name of the Lord; for concerning this also the Lord has said, "Give not that which is holy to the dogs." (ch. 9)

Ignatius, Bishop of Antioch, writes:

They abstain from the Eucharist and from prayer, because they confess not the Eucharist to be the flesh of our Saviour Jesus Christ, which suffered for our sins, and which the Father, of His goodness, raised up again. Those, therefore, who speak against this gift of God, incur death in the midst of their disputes. (Smyrnaeans, ch. 7)

I have confidence of you in the Lord, that ye will be of no other mind. Wherefore I write boldly to your love, which is worthy of God, and exhort you to have but one faith, and one [kind of] preaching, and one Eucharist. For there is one flesh of the Lord Jesus Christ; and His blood which was shed for us is one; one loaf also is broken to all, and one cup is distributed among them all: there is but one altar for the whole Church, and one bishop, with the presbytery and deacons, my fellow-servants. (Philadelphians, ch. 4)

Obey the bishop and the presbytery with an undivided mind, breaking one and the same bread, which is the

*medicine of immortality, and the antidote to prevent us
from dying, but [which causes] that we should live for ever
in Jesus Christ. (Ephesians, ch. 20)*

Justin the Martyr (martyred near 165) writes:

*And this food is called among us Eucharist, of which no
one is allowed to partake but the man who believes that
the things which we teach are true, and who has been
washed with the washing that is for the remission of sins,
and unto regeneration, and who is so living as Christ has
enjoined. For not as common bread and common drink
do we receive these; but in like manner as Jesus Christ our
Saviour, having been made flesh by the Word of God, had
both flesh and blood for our salvation, so likewise have we
been taught that the food which is blessed by the prayer of
His word, and from which our blood and flesh by transmu-
tation are nourished, is the flesh and blood of that Jesus
who was made flesh. (First Apology, ch. 66)*

Alone these may not seem like much, but they are in
fact among the first Christian documents outside the New
Testament, written by those who were near to the Apostles.
Most of these documents were also circulated at the same time
as the Gospels and Epistles of Paul to the various Christian
communities. If any of these writers had taught false doctrines,
it is reasonable to expect that the writings would have been
quickly condemned, just as every other heretical document
and false teaching was condemned up to that point. Yet here
we find just the opposite. These writings are received with ease
and transmitted to the general Christian community for the
teaching and edification of all.

These passages, in addition to the plain, straightforward, and literal reading of the New Testament and a study of the Apostolic Church's practice for two thousand years, make it abundantly clear that no alternate reading of the New Testament should be considered sound or true. As contemporary Orthodox theologian Georges Florovsky said, "Tradition is Scripture, rightly understood."

If the average Protestant and evangelical church has incorrectly understood one of the clearest, most biblical, and most well-documented Christian doctrines, how can we trust them to give sound scriptural guidance regarding any subject? The cost of such a misunderstanding of these subjects is a human one. It is unfulfilled and undeveloped Christians who are the victims.

Many groups have brought on these troubles by continually reinventing themselves in order to draw in the masses, or by simply reading the Bible incorrectly. These churches starve their children spiritually because they withhold the bread of life. They do this by reinventing the teachings that have been faithfully passed down by the Church. It is no wonder at all that people are leaving the mainline denominations in droves. If the sheep haven't been fed, they look for greener pastures.

Before concluding this section, let's look at an interesting passage on the subject of the Eucharist in *The Oxford Dictionary of the Christian Church*:

> *In the Patristic period there was remarkably little in the way of controversy on the subject. . . . That the Eucharist conveyed to the believer the Body and Blood of Christ was universally accepted from the first, and language was*

very commonly used which referred to the Eucharistic elements as themselves the Body and Blood. Even where the elements were spoken of as 'symbols' or 'antitypes' there was no intention of denying the reality of the Presence in the gifts....

The first controversies on the nature of the Eucharistic Presence date from the earlier Middle Ages. In the 9th century Paschasius Radbertus raised doubts as to the identity of Christ's Eucharistic Body... but won practically no support. (pp. 475–476)

Whether we like it or not, we've been shortchanged spiritually. It might have been by a pastor or teacher who meant well and interpreted the passages in the best way he could using practical, earthly reasoning, or it might have been by someone who never questioned the denominational confession or party line. Either way, we have missed out on something so important to the early Christians that they partook of it every single time they came together, especially on Sundays.

As we return again to Acts we read, "And they continued steadfastly in the apostles' doctrine and fellowship, in the breaking of bread, and in prayers" (Acts 2:42). This is what Christians did when they got together on Sundays. It was in the breaking of the bread that they met the Lord Jesus and communed with Him in quite a literal sense: "He who eats My flesh and drinks My blood abides in Me, and I in him" (John 6:56).

The Lord Jesus becomes the very center of our lives as we hear His words in the Gospel and then partake thankfully of His Body and Blood in a mystical and spiritual way. He unites us to one another because we each share His one Body and His Blood in one cup. Could any experience be more joyful or more fulfilling than to be filled with the presence of the One who is the source of life?

7

Holy Baptism & Chrismation

There are many passages throughout the New Testament that speak about baptism. Let's look at a few of the passages as well as the teaching of the early Christians and that of the Orthodox Church.

Baptism comes from the Greek word *baptiso* (meaning "to dunk"). In some churches the act of baptism is in fact a dunking or full immersion in water, while others practice only sprinkling (also known as "aspersion"). Many Protestant denominations teach that the act of being baptized is a symbolic one, simply an outward sign of an inward decision to receive Christ into your life as Lord and Savior. But again we have to ask where they got such an idea. As you are about to see, that line of thinking is not present in the New Testament or the early writings of the Church.

Paul writes, "Or do you not know that as many of us as were baptized into Christ Jesus were baptized into His death?

Therefore we were buried with Him through baptism into death, that just as Christ was raised from the dead by the glory of the Father, even so we also should walk in newness of life" (Rom. 6:3–4). We don't see any symbolic language but the expectation of a new reality. Baptism is not merely a symbol; it grants us a special gift from God. This gift is burial and death with Christ in order that we might be resurrected with Him.

In Mark, the Lord Jesus says to His disciples, "He who believes and is baptized will be saved" (Mark 16:16a). It is interesting again to note that for the Lord Jesus, baptism is in fact a necessity. How many symbols do you know of that are a necessity? If the Lord is equating baptism with salvation, it must be very important.

Again in John we see the Lord teaching about baptism when He speaks with Nicodemus:

> *Jesus answered and said to him, "Most assuredly, I say to you, unless one is born again, he cannot see the kingdom of God." Nicodemus said to Him, "How can a man be born when he is old? Can he enter a second time into his mother's womb and be born?" Jesus answered, "Most assuredly, I say to you, unless one is born of water and the Spirit, he cannot enter the kingdom of God." (John 3:3–5)*

Again we see that water and spirit are two sides of the same coin and that coin can't be divided, according to the Lord.

But what happens to all the people who die before they are baptized?

The answer here is a mystery. We don't know what happens to those who don't receive baptism, but we are comforted by two facts: that God is both loving and merciful. We know that He cares for us and has a plan for each of us. Instead of focusing on the what-ifs or speculating, we can focus on the things that have been clearly revealed by the Lord while there is still a chance for our lives to be changed for the better.

Returning to the necessity of baptism, let us hear the words of the Apostle Peter on the Day of Pentecost:

> *Then Peter said to them, "Repent, and let every one of you be baptized in the name of Jesus Christ for the remission of sins; and you shall receive the gift of the Holy Spirit. For the promise is to you and to your children, and to all who are afar off, as many as the Lord our God will call. . . . Then those who gladly received his word were baptized; and that day about three thousand souls were added to them. (Acts 2:38–39, 41)*

Again we see that they are told to be baptized. In fact it was so important that even though there were three thousand who came to faith in Christ that day, the Apostles did not say, "Well, there are too many of you here today, and since baptism is simply a symbol we'll go ahead and skip it." We notice St. Peter clearly teaching that "the promise is to you and to your children." He also teaches the people that baptism is for the "remission of sins." This is seen in many places, including Acts 22, when Ananias says to Paul, "And now why are you waiting? Arise and be baptized, and wash away your sins" (Acts 22:16). No symbolic baptism could ever do such a thing!

Here are a few other quotations that demonstrate the early Christian understanding of the sacrament of Baptism.

Origen, scholar and theologian from Alexandria, Egypt (184–254):

The Church received from the apostles the tradition of giving baptism even to infants. The apostles, to whom were committed the secrets of divine sacraments, knew there is in everyone innate strains of sin, which must be washed away through water and the Spirit. (Commentaries on Romans 5:9)

Ambrose, Bishop of Milan (340–397):

The Church was redeemed at the price of Christ's blood. Jew or Greek, it makes no difference; but if he has believed, he must circumcise himself from his sins [in baptism (Col. 2:11–12)] so that he can be saved . . . for no one ascends into the kingdom of heaven except through the sacrament of baptism. . . . "Unless a man be born again of water and the Holy Spirit, he cannot enter the kingdom of God." (On Abraham 2:11:79–84)

THE GIFT OF THE HOLY SPIRIT

A study of baptism leads us to another problem with this doctrine in most Protestant denominations. According to Acts, baptism alone does not grant the gift of the Holy Spirit:

Now when the apostles who were at Jerusalem heard that Samaria had received the word of God, they sent Peter and John to them, who, when they had come down, prayed for them that they might receive the Holy Spirit. For as yet He had fallen upon none of them. They had only been baptized in the name of the Lord Jesus. Then they laid hands on them, and they received the Holy Spirit. (Acts 8:14–17)

The passage continues to reinforce the idea in the next verses: "And when Simon saw that through the laying on of the apostles' hands the Holy Spirit was given, he offered them money, saying, 'Give me this power also, that anyone on whom I lay hands may receive the Holy Spirit'" (Acts 8:18–19).

So, amazingly, we see that it wasn't enough simply to be baptized. Again we see the role of the sacramental priesthood in the work of the Apostles as they came to lay hands on the newly baptized.

After the Apostles died, the teaching of the Orthodox Church is that they passed on the tradition of the sacrament of chrism. Chrism (also known as *myron*) is a special oil of anointing that was originally blessed by the Apostles. In modern times, it is blessed only by the patriarchs or heads of the various Orthodox churches at specifically appointed times. It is even possible John the Evangelist is speaking about this in his first general epistle when he writes, "But you have an anointing from the Holy One, and you know all things" (1 John 2:20). A few verses later he also writes:

> But the anointing which you have received from Him abides in you, and you do not need that anyone teach you; but as the same anointing teaches you concerning all things, and is true, and is not a lie, and just as it has taught you, you will abide in Him. (v. 27)

This anointing is spoken of throughout the early centuries of Christianity. The early Christian writer Tertullian (160–225), who connects the sacrament to Old Testament practice, has this to say:

Then having gone up from the bath we are anointed with a blessed anointing of ancient discipline, by which people were accustomed to be anointed for priesthood, by oil from a horn from which Aaron was anointed by Moses (Ex 30:22–30). For this reason we were called "christs" (anointed ones) from "chrism," which is the ointment which lends its name to the Lord.

Hippolytus, a Roman priest (170–235), writes:

The neophytes are anointed by the presbyter from the oil consecrated by the bishop. He says, 'I anoint you with holy oil in the name of Jesus Christ.' (Apostolic Tradition 21–22)

Cyril, Bishop of Jerusalem (313–386), writes:

And to you in like manner, after you had come up from the pool of the sacred streams, there was given an Unction, the anti-type of that wherewith Christ was anointed; and this is the Holy Spirit. (Catechetical Lecture 21:1)

Basil, Bishop of Caeserea (330–379), one of the great figures of Christian history, has this to say:

We also bless the water of baptism, the oil of anointing, and even the baptized themselves. By virtue of what writings? Is it not by virtue of the protected, secret, and hidden tradition? Indeed! Even the oil of anointing, what written word has taught about that? The triple immersion, from where does it come? And everything that surrounds baptism: the renunciation of Satan and his angels—from what scripture does that come? Is it not from that teaching held private and secret, which our fathers kept in silence, protected from anxiety and curiosity, knowing well that in keeping quiet one safeguards the sacred character of the mysteries? For how would it be reasonable to divulge by writing the instruction, that which is not permitted to the uninitiated to contemplate? (On the Holy Spirit 15, 35)

Not only does St. Basil show us the teaching about the sacrament of chrism, but we also see him touch on the subject of holy tradition and why certain subjects are not "divulged by writings" but kept secret and safe from "the uninitiated"—that is, those who have not yet received Christian baptism. This was all the more important when we remember that Christians had many enemies, such as the various pagan groups.

Since this sacrament of the early Christians has fallen out of practice in nearly every church besides the Orthodox and in some instances the Roman Catholic, we are forced to ask a couple of questions. First, how do we know that we have received the Holy Spirit when it is clear that one can be baptized without receiving it? Second, if we have not received the Holy Spirit through chrismation, then what are we waiting for? God wants to bless our lives. Why let others take away our blessings through subtle theological and doctrinal changes? This is the way that has been preserved for us from apostolic times. If we feel like our walk with Christ is missing something, is it possible that we are missing the anointing of the Holy Spirit, the sacrament of chrism?

8

A Life of Confession

Perhaps one of the most hotly debated yet least understood sacraments is confession. Let's take some time to unwrap this mystery a bit.

Confession is the practice of coming in repentance before a priest and pouring out your sins and faults to Jesus Christ. At the conclusion of the confession, the priest may give a few words of advice or encouragement, depending on what the individual might need. As he concludes, the priest prays over the person and offers absolution as a minister of the forgiveness of Jesus Christ.

Most Protestant denominations believe the practice of confessing to any human is unbiblical since "there is one God and one Mediator between God and men, the Man Christ Jesus" (1 Tim. 2:5). Interestingly enough, some Protestants, such as Lutherans, still have the ability to perform this rite, though it has generally fallen out of practice.

Many people believe they could never confess to another human being. Before we go any further, let's remember we are not interested in being part of a church that has the teachings we like the most. We are interested in finding the church with the true teachings of Jesus Christ and His Apostles. Is confession a Roman Catholic invention used to promote the power of the hierarchy, or could it be a God-ordained, powerful aid for our spiritual struggle?

In a number of passages, the New Testament speaks about confession and the absolution of sins, both as general ideas and as a sacramental mystery: "So Jesus said to them again, 'Peace to you! As the Father has sent Me, I also send you.' And when He had said this, He breathed on them, and said to them, 'Receive the Holy Spirit. If you forgive the sins of any, they are forgiven them; if you retain the sins of any, they are retained'" (John 20:21–23).

We see here that the Lord Himself breathed the Holy Spirit onto the disciples for the purpose of passing on one of the great gifts of His ministry, the gift of forgiving sins and transgressions. This was a sort of ordination of the disciples. When men or women tell us that only God can forgive, then we should ask them what exactly is meant by this verse. It seems clear to the Orthodox and to the early Church that this is a special gift given to Christ's own ministers. "Confess *your* trespasses to one another, and pray for one another, that you may be healed. The effective, fervent prayer of a righteous man avails much" (James 5:16). "If we confess our sins, He is faithful and just to forgive us *our* sins and to cleanse us from all unrighteousness" (1 John 1:9).

It is well known that in the early Church confession was a public act performed before all the members of the community.

This was quite an important aspect of worship because each person's salvation was seen as wrapped up and completely bound with that of their fellow Christians. When one man sinned, whether openly or in private, it was seen as harmful to the community as a whole. However, it seems the practice of general confession in the church fell out of use in favor of a confession made in person with a priest as witness.

The reason this changed was in order to help people who might have felt an overwhelming sense of shame in having to open up before the community. Of course, certain sins would also have created a great sense of scandal within the community. It might, for instance, lead to gossip and judging or condemnation, as so often happens when humans enter the equation. Sadly, the gift provided by the Lord to remove sin might have been a stumbling block to others. So the priest was chosen to hear the sins on behalf of the people.

This was the logical solution for a number of reasons. First, the priest is the only one within a community (aside from the bishop) who could absolve sins. Second, the confession to the priest meant the sins were kept secret and safe, as the priests observe a seal of confession. Third, the time with a priest allows a relationship to develop on the spiritual level. This relationship can help a priest find meaningful ways of giving counsel and correction to the confessing individual in order to help him or her stay the course. Fourth, confession before another human being proves the individual is indeed repentant and humble enough to come forward and allow another to know his or her secrets. This type of humility is the key to spiritual success.

Here is what a few of the early Church writings had to say about this sacrament.

"*Confess your sins in church, and do not go up to your prayer with an evil conscience.*" *(Didache, 4:14)*

Some of these women make a public confession, but others are ashamed to do this, and in silence, as if withdrawing from themselves the hope of life in God, they either apostatize entirely or hesitate between two courses. (Irenaeus, Against Heresies, 1:22)

[Regarding confession, some] flee from this work as being an exposure of themselves, or they put it off from day to day. I presume they are more mindful of modesty than of salvation, like those who contract a disease in the more shameful parts of the body and shun making themselves known to the physicians; and thus they perish along with their own bashfulness. [Tertullian, Repentance, 10:1]

[A brotherly method of forgiveness], albeit hard and difficult [is] the remission of sins through penance, when the sinner . . . does not shrink from declaring his sin to a priest of the Lord and from seeking medicine. (Origen, Homilies in Leviticus, 2:4)

Of how much greater faith and fear are they who . . . confess their sins to the priests of God in a straightforward manner and in sorrow, making an open declaration of conscience. . . . I beseech you, brethren; let everyone who has sinned confess his sin while he is still in this world, while his confession is still admissible, while the satisfaction and remission made through the priests are still pleasing before the Lord. (Cyprian, Bishop of Carthage [251], On the Lapsed, ch. 28)

> *Priests have received a power which God has given neither to angels nor to archangels. It was said to them: "Whatsoever you shall bind on earth shall be bound in heaven; and whatsoever you shall loose, shall be loosed." Temporal rulers have indeed the power of binding: but they can only bind the body. Priests, in contrast, can bind with a bond which pertains to the soul itself and transcends the very heavens. (John Chrysostom, On the Priesthood, 3:5)*

We've seen the scriptural references as well as some quotations from a veritable "Who's Who" of the early Church. Again, keep in mind that these writers were all well-respected sources of teaching for the Church. We would also do well to remember that we regularly pay good money to specialists such as counselors, psychologists, and psychiatrists in order for them to hear our confessions—in a manner of speaking. As the well-known writer G. K. Chesterton once said, "Psychoanalysis is confession without absolution." In many cases these professionals might give us help such as processing and coping techniques or medicine, but as Christians we never forget that Jesus Christ gave His Apostles true medicine to bind wounds and to heal the many diseases caused by sin.

Repentance is not simply an act that takes place once in the life of a Christian. It is an ongoing way of life that is necessary in the daily pursuit of the Christian way, because only the pure in heart shall see God (Matt. 5:8). This way of life pushes us toward God through confession. If we have been attending church all our life yet still find ourselves struggling with past sins and the guilt they bring, perhaps we might benefit from receiving the medicine of absolution. Christ our Lord wanted each of us to have this gift. "Let us lay aside every weight, and the sin which so easily ensnares *us*, and let us run with endurance the race that is set before us" (Heb. 12:1).

9

Unction of the Sick

Unction or anointing of the sick is a sacramental practice of the Church that was already well known by the time of the writing of the New Testament. So it is today in the Orthodox Church that whenever someone is sick, a priest or a group of priests along with other believers will visit the sick individual and pray for him or her, while also blessing oil that will be used for anointing.

Mark the evangelist writes, "And they cast out many demons, and anointed with oil many who were sick, and healed them" (Mark 6:13). We notice in the passage according to Mark that this practice originated from the teaching of the Lord Jesus. Regarding the anointing, the Apostle James also writes,

Is anyone among you sick? Let him call for the elders of the church, and let them pray over him, anointing him with oil in the name of the Lord. And the prayer of faith will

save the sick, and the Lord will raise him up. And if he has committed sins, he will be forgiven. Confess your trespasses to one another, and pray for one another, that you may be healed. (James 5:14–16)

We see that when someone is sick within the Christian community, he is told to call for the elders (which we now understand to mean presbyters). This anointing was initially meant to be done by a group of presbyters, and as we can see, there is a relationship between the anointing and the confession of sins. This is true because we as Christians believe that sin causes mental and physical as well as spiritual harm. The connection between sin and illness is quite scriptural, as seen in the following example: "Afterward Jesus found him in the temple, and said to him, 'See, you have been made well. Sin no more, lest a worse thing come upon you'" (John 5:14).

Below are a few quotes from the early Church regarding this subject.

Serapion, Bishop of Thmuis, Egypt (reposed 360):

We beseech you, Savior of all men, you that have all virtue and power, Father of our Lord and Savior Jesus Christ, and we pray that you send down from heaven the healing power of the only-begotten [Son] upon this oil, so that for those who are anointed . . . it may be effected for the casting out of every disease and every bodily infirmity . . . for good grace and remission of sins. (The Sacramentary of Serapion 29:1)

Caesarius, Bishop of Arles, France (470–543):

As often as some infirmity overtakes a man, let him who is ill receive the body and blood of Christ; let him humbly and

in faith ask the presbyters for blessed oil, to anoint his body,
so that what was written may be fulfilled in him: "Is anyone
among you sick? Let him bring in the presbyters, and let
them pray over him, anointing him with oil; and the prayer
of faith will save the sick man, and the Lord will raise him
up; and if he be in sins, they will be forgiven him."... See to
it, brethren, that whoever is ill hasten to the church, both
that he may receive health of body and will merit to obtain
the forgiveness of his sins. (Sermons 13:3)

Sickness is often allowed by God in order to bring us to repentance and to give us a prayerful mindset. We must, however, remember that God has given us medicines for the healing of body and soul since He is the Savior of both. These medicines are obtained from the hospital of God, the Church. They are administered by the physicians of God, the clergy, in order to bring wholeness and health to the man, woman, or child who asks for forgiveness and healing from the depths of his heart.

10

Holy Matrimony

Holy matrimony is the sacrament that unites a man and woman in marriage. This is conducted by a priest, usually in the presence of many witnesses. Among other things, this sacrament reminds us of the marriage bond between the Lord Jesus and His Bride the Church (Eph. 5).

The service itself contains many features not typically present in mainline Protestant weddings, such as a betrothal service and a crowning of the husband and wife, which symbolizes that we as Christians are royalty grafted into the royal family of Jesus Christ. The crowns also remind us that the husband and wife will be king and queen of their household.

The service continues with the husband and wife sharing a common cup of wine. This is symbolic of the mystery of marriage in that each spouse must help the other in drinking whatever life sets before them. Whether it be sweet or bitter, they must taste of it together. Marriage is the cup God the

Father sets before them, and He fully expects them to drink of this cup. The rite of matrimony concludes with a procession while holding hands, in which the husband and wife take their first steps together as a married couple.

One conspicuously absent feature in Orthodox weddings is the idea of vows, whether handwritten or formal. The Church recognizes that human vows have little value and are broken quite often, especially in our society. Instead the Church prays for the couple and asks God to bless them in the way He blessed many couples throughout the Old and New Testaments. We pray the new couple will be faithful to this form of "martyrdom" and learn to die to themselves and their selfish desires in order to fully grow in love for each other and for the Lord.

In the Orthodox Church, as in Scripture, the only marriage that is considered holy is the marriage of one man to one woman. Any marriage that does not meet this requirement is considered outside of the will of God for our lives, as the Lord Himself teaches: "But from the beginning of the creation, God 'made them male and female. . . . For this reason a man shall leave his father and mother and be joined to his wife, and the two shall become one flesh'; so then they are no longer two, but one flesh" (Mark 10:6–8).

The only acceptable alternative to entering into a marriage of one man and one woman is to live a completely chaste and pure life as a single person.

Divorce, while not recommended in most cases, is allowed in some circumstances, such as instances of abuse or adultery. Remarriage is also allowed by the Church. It is not considered an ideal scenario, but the Church in her wisdom and mercy does not want those who have suffered through divorce to suffer further by being tempted into sinful, unchaste lives while also being ostracized from the rest of the Church community. Out of concern for her children, the Church allows them to marry again and attempt to live holy and pure lives that are well-pleasing to God.

Here are a couple of quotes regarding marriage from the early Church:

> *The union should be made with the consent of the bishop, so that the marriage may be according to the Lord and not merely out of lust. (Ignatius of Antioch, Letter to Polycarp)*

> *The love of husband and wife is the force that welds society together. (John Chrysostom, Homily on Ephesians 5:33)*

Marriage is a special relationship of growth and maturity through the work of the Holy Spirit. That growth between a man and a woman occurs on a mental, physical, and spiritual level. Contrary to some other churches, the Orthodox Church does not believe marriage was designed only for the purpose of creating children. There is more to marriage than offspring. While children are a great blessing, the main purpose of marriage is to reflect the reality of the marriage of Christ to His Church. If God is truly a part of our marriage, it becomes a way to our salvation through selfless, sacrificial love.

11

The Angelic Life

One of the areas where the Orthodox Church differs quite a bit from Protestant denominations is in the life of monasticism. Monasticism is a form of religious life that is usually centered around communal prayer and work as part of a group of like-minded people, a community.

This way of life is undertaken by men and women all over the world who have such a zeal for God that they have no intention to live out their lives in a common or conventional way. These folks don't want to find a spouse, raise children, or secure a grand old nest egg for retirement. Ordinarily this might pose quite a problem to an individual because the temptations of the world could prove too strong. However, the monastic community of monks or nuns becomes a safe haven for those who truly love God and want to fully "work out [their] salvation with fear and trembling" (Phil. 2:12), while detaching themselves from the world. The community of brothers or sisters becomes the family and the support system of the man or woman who decides to dedicate his or her life completely to the communal life of prayer. Typically the virtues of poverty, chastity (celibacy), and obedience are taken as lifelong vows by the one who enters into such a community.

While Christian monasticism did not officially begin until the third century, we see that throughout the Scriptures there are many examples of men and women who lived quite similarly to monks and nuns. This includes many of the prophets of the Old Testament, such as Elijah and Elisha. Other examples of this lifestyle in the Bible include the apostle Paul, John the Baptist and Forerunner of Christ, and Anna the prophetess in the Gospel of Luke. The Bible gives us some insight into this form of Christian life.

> *His disciples said to Him, "If such is the case of the man with* his *wife, it is better not to marry." But He said to them, "All cannot accept this saying, but only* those *to whom it has been given: For there are eunuchs* who were born thus from* their *mother's womb, and there are eunuchs who were made eunuchs by men, and there are eunuchs who have made themselves eunuchs for the kingdom of heaven's sake. He who is able to accept* it, *let him accept* it. *(Matt. 19:10–12)*

> *Jesus said to him, "If you want to be perfect, go, sell what you have and give to the poor, and you will have treasure in heaven; and come, follow Me." (Matt. 19:21)*

---

* This word is used by the Lord to describe a celibate individual.

But I say this as a concession, not as a commandment. For I wish that all men were even as I myself. But each one has his own gift from God, one in this manner and another in that. But I say to the unmarried and to the widows: It is good for them if they remain even as I am; but if they cannot exercise self-control, let them marry. For it is better to marry than to burn with passion. *(1 Cor. 7:6–9)*

But I want you to be without care. He who is unmarried cares for the things of the Lord—how he may please the Lord. But he who is married cares about the things of the world—how he may please his *wife. There is a difference between a wife and a virgin. The unmarried woman cares about the things of the Lord, that she may be holy both in body and in spirit. But she who is married cares about the things of the world—how she may please* her *husband. And this I say for your own profit, not that I may put a leash on you, but for what is proper, and that you may serve the Lord without distraction. (1 Cor. 7:32–35)*

Of course we're reminded that the Lord Jesus lived in this manner during His earthly ministry. He led a group of faithful followers and lived in chastity and poverty while also in obedience to God the Father. He typically spent His time either working or praying. Often we are told of His time spent alone in prayer.

The man regarded as the father of Christian monasticism is Anthony of Egypt (also known as Anthony the Great). His life was written down for us by Athanasius, Archbishop of Alexandria (the same man who helped decide the final compilation of books that were included in the New Testament). Since his time in the third century, many thousands of faithful men and women have taken the leap of forsaking the world in order to live more fully for Christ. Here are a few quotes about the monastic life from the early centuries of Christianity.

> *Virginity is better than marriage, however good. . . . Celibacy is . . . an imitation of the angels. Therefore, virginity is as much more honorable than marriage, as the angel is higher than man. But why do I say angel? Christ, Himself, is the glory of virginity. (John Chrysostom, Homily 19 on First Corinthians[3])*

> *For by this time there are monasteries among you, and the name of monk receives public recognition. (Athanasius, Prologue, Life of Anthony[4])*

John Cassian, monk and theologian (360–435):

> *[St. Basil, bishop of Cappadocia] is reported once to have said to a senator, who had renounced the world in a half-hearted manner and was keeping back some of his personal fortune: "you have lost the senator and failed to make a monk." . . . This uprooting [of greed] is difficult to achieve unless we are living in a monastery, for in a monastery we cease to worry about even our most basic needs. (On Avarice)[5]*

The monastic life and its development are very important aspects in the history of the Christian Church. Throughout history the monasteries have been seen as centers of spirituality that give great support and encouragement to those who visit.

Monasteries also support the entire Church and, in fact, the world through the prayers of the holy ones who have dedicated their lives to this purpose, for "the effective, fervent prayer of a righteous man avails much" (James 5:16).

Having a tradition of monasticism gives us tools and examples for our own spiritual disciplines and the struggles that accompany them. The monks and nuns teach us how to pray more deeply and converse more fully with the Lord Jesus Christ by learning to renounce the world, as John tells us: "Do not love the world or the things in the world" (1 John 2:15). They also show us that prayer *is* work—and as in the story of Mary and Martha of Bethany, Orthodox monastics have "chosen that good part, which will not be taken away" (Luke 10:42). While many talk about loving God, these holy men and women show us what it means to do so more perfectly through a life of holy dedication: self-denial, physical labor, and ceaseless prayer.

12

Mary and the Cloud of Witnesses

When we say the word *saint,* people immediately have a picture in mind, a thought about what that actually means. In the New Testament, the word *saint* is generally used to speak of anyone in the Christian community. For example, we see the apostle Paul frequently writing to "the saints" of the various churches. The words for *saint* and *holy* are in fact interchangeable in many languages, such as Latin and Greek (the language of the New Testament).

In the Orthodox Church, every Christian is a saint. This is true because each Christian has been set apart and made holy, especially through baptism and chrismation. However, we also have a tradition of "glorifying" or "canonizing" saints—that is, we write their names in a list (a *canon*). As a Church, we find there are some people who have been such models of the Christian life and have reflected the love of God and His glory in such a dramatic way as to be honored universally by the Church even after their departure from this earthly life.

This type of veneration is evident even in the secular world, as we see with the monuments in places such as Washington, D.C., as well as the faces of past presidents on our currency. Such items are dedicated to different presidents and leaders of our land, people who embodied what it meant to be an American. These men often went to their death in service of their country. While thousands of people visit these monuments every year, at no point do we think of the visitors as idol worshipers. We simply call them "patriotic."

When we speak of canonized saints, we are speaking of those honored by the Church for their contributions to Christianity or for their faith and holiness. The apostle Paul writes:

Therefore we also, since we are surrounded by so great a cloud of witnesses, let us lay aside every weight, and the sin which so easily ensnares us, and let us run with endurance the race that is set before us, looking unto Jesus, the author and finisher of our faith. (Heb. 12:1–2)

And we desire that each one of you show the same diligence to the full assurance of hope until the end, that you do not become sluggish, but imitate those who through faith and patience inherit the promises. (Heb. 6:11–12)

Even though Paul was one of the early Christians, he already understood the idea of a "cloud of witnesses." He saw these witnesses as models of the patience, perseverance, and faith that are needed to endure that long marathon called the Christian life.

No conversation about the saints is complete without speaking about the greatest saint in the history of the world, the

Virgin Mary. She not only made history, but her decision to be obedient to God's will helped redeem it.

The Orthodox Church differs from most churches because we honor the Virgin Mary above all other mere humans. Contrary to the beliefs of some, the Orthodox do not consider the Virgin to be a savior, a co-redeemer, another member of the Holy Trinity, or any such thing. We do, however, fully understand the reality of the matter. Out of all the women who have ever lived throughout the history of the world in every time and place, God chose her. She was probably not more than twelve or fourteen years old, and yet God chose her. We read this in Luke:

And having come in, the angel said to her, "Rejoice, highly favored one, *the Lord* is *with you; blessed are you among women!" But when she saw* him, *she was troubled at his saying, and considered what manner of greeting this was. Then the angel said to her, "Do not be afraid, Mary, for you have found favor with God. And behold, you will conceive in your womb and bring forth a Son, and shall call His name Jesus. He will be great, and will be called the Son of the Highest; and the Lord God will give Him the throne of His father David. And He will reign over the house of Jacob forever, and of His kingdom there will be no end." Then Mary said to the angel, "How can this be, since I do not know a man?" And the angel answered and said to her, "The Holy Spirit will come upon you, and the power of the Highest will overshadow you; therefore, also, that Holy One who is to be born will be called the Son of God. Now indeed, Elizabeth your relative has also conceived a son in her old age; and this is now the sixth month for her who was called barren. For with God nothing will be impossible." Then*

Mary said, "Behold the maidservant of the Lord! Let it be to me according to your word." And the angel departed from her. (Luke 1:28–38)

While we read in Genesis that Eve was tempted into disobedience, the Virgin Mary humbly accepted the will of God. Contrary to the beliefs of some churches, we do not believe God simply could have chosen another. God doesn't compromise: He chose the greatest of all women and no other. And fortunately for our sakes, despite the horrible pressures it would bring and the risks involved, she accepted.

The Orthodox Church does not view the Virgin simply as some sort of a tunnel that Jesus Christ passed through on His way to becoming human. In Orthodox belief, it is Mary who gives Jesus His human nature. They share the same human DNA! And without human DNA, there would be no humanity in the Lord Jesus. This humanity was (and is) complete in every way. Without the complete and full humanity of Jesus, there would be no significance to the Crucifixion and death He endured for each of us.

It is no wonder, then, that she is called "Mother of God," since she gave birth to God in the flesh. To put her into some perspective, let's look at a passage from the Old Testament:

And when they came to Chidon's threshing floor, Uzzah put out his hand to take hold of the ark, for the oxen stumbled. Then the anger of the LORD was kindled against Uzzah, and He struck him down because he put out his hand to the ark, and he died there before God. (1 Chr. 13:9–10)

In this passage we see that a man who meant well was struck dead for simply touching the ark of the covenant.

That ark was very special since it contained the Law of God, the Ten Commandments. If this ark was holy and untouchable in the eyes of God because it held tablets made of stone, written by God, imagine how much more sacred and precious the Virgin Mary must be, who carried the Son of God Himself in her womb! The two are not even comparable. The Virgin Mary is indeed quite special, for, as she said, "behold, henceforth all generations will call me blessed" (Luke 1:48).

In the Orthodox Church we ask for the intercessions of the Virgin Mary and other saints. We are often mischaracterized as praying to the saints or worshiping the saints, but nothing could be further from the truth. Asking the saints to intercede for us is simply talking to the saints as to friends and asking them to pray for us. For anyone who thinks that such asking is wrong, we might wonder if they have ever asked someone to pray for them. I have often asked others to pray for me, especially during times of particular need, and I'm sure that is common for most of us.

If you believe asking the prayers of a living person is different from asking the prayers of a dead one, consider the words of the Lord Jesus: "'I am the God of Abraham, the God of Isaac, and the God of Jacob'? God is not the God of the dead, but of the living" (Matt. 22:32).

It should surprise us that the Lord refers to Abraham, Isaac, and Jacob, who died long ago, not as simply dead. Quite the opposite, in fact—the Lord tells us God is the God of the living! That might shock us, but there is a secret hidden within those words. The secret is that those who die in Christ live in Him. When someone who has been well-pleasing to God is taken from this life, he or she does not simply go to the grave. The physical body rests in the grave, but the soul of the righteous lives. Paul writes:

> *For none of us lives to himself, and no one dies to himself. For if we live, we live to the Lord; and if we die, we die to the Lord. Therefore, whether we live or die, we are the Lord's. For to this end Christ died and rose and lived again, that He might be Lord of both the dead and the living. (Rom. 14:7–9)*

The Lord Jesus also says, "I am the resurrection and the life. He who believes in Me, though he may die, he shall live. And whoever lives and believes in Me shall never die" (John 11:25–26). It is this understanding of the death of the righteous that makes us quite comfortable reaching out and conversing with the saints. Even the Lord Jesus was seen doing this when He was visited by Moses and Elijah on Mount Tabor, as seen in Matthew 17, Mark 9, and Luke 9.

We do not pray to the dead and ask them to change our fortunes or tell us the future. We simply speak to the saints, asking them to pray for us, in a way that is similar to asking our friends or our church family to pray for us. This makes sense for Orthodox Christians because saints are part of our family in Christ. In the Scriptures we are told that "precious in the sight of the LORD / Is the death of His saints" (Psalm 116:15). It is precious to Him because they are His and He loves them. It is because He loves them that He continues to hear their prayers on our behalf, since prayer is an act of love.

Here are a few words regarding the saints from the early centuries of Christianity:

In this way is he [the true Christian] always pure for prayer. He also prays in the society of angels, as being already of angelic rank, and he is never out of their holy keeping; and though he pray alone, he has the choir of the saints standing with him [in prayer]. (Clement of Alexandria, Miscellanies 7:12)

Let us remember one another in concord and unanimity. Let us on both sides [of death] always pray for one another. Let us relieve burdens and afflictions by mutual love. (Cyprian of Carthage, Letters 56[60]:5)

When you perceive that God is chastening you, fly not to his enemies . . . but to his friends, the martyrs, the saints, and those who were pleasing to him, and who have great power [in God]. (John Chrysostom, Orations 8:6)

Yes, I am well assured that [my father's] intercession is of more avail now than was his instruction in former days, since he is closer to God, now that he has shaken off his bodily fetters, and freed his mind from the clay that obscured it. (Gregory the Theologian, Orations 18:4)

You say in your book that while we live we are able to pray for each other, but afterwards when we have died, the prayer of no person for another can be heard. . . . But if the Apostles and martyrs while still in the body can pray for others, at a time when they ought still be solicitous [concerned] about themselves, how much more will they do so after their crowns, victories, and triumphs? (Jerome, Against Vigilantius 6)

A Christian people celebrates together in religious solemnity the memorials of the martyrs, both to encourage their being imitated and so that it can share in their merits and be aided by their prayers. (Augustine, Against Faustus the Manichean)

Here again we have the privilege of seeing the Church and the Bible through the eyes of the best and brightest leaders of the early Church. If we want to grow deeper in the life of Christ, we will always be challenged to put our old assumptions aside and open ourselves up to greater possibilities. For these men, death was nothing more than a speed bump; members of the body of Christ remained members in full standing even after departing from this life. Perhaps we need the faith to realize that Christ has truly conquered death and given us the chance to be His saints even beyond the grave. "For I am persuaded that neither death nor life . . . shall be able to separate us from the love of God which is in Christ Jesus our Lord" (Rom. 8:38–39).

13

The Physical Life

Often in the life of a Christian there is a great emphasis on "the Spirit," or spirituality, or some vague variation thereof. While an Orthodox Christian also thinks about the spiritual life, there is something more to it. There is a physical side to being spiritual. From how we eat to our posture in prayer, there are many physical, tangible elements to our life in Christ. That makes perfect sense since Jesus Christ Himself took flesh and became a physical reality in the world for each and every one of us.

Because of the Fall, our physical self and our spiritual self are out of sorts. Our physical self is soaked in sin and expresses desires that are contrary to the desires of the spirit, just as the apostle Paul writes: "For the flesh lusts against the Spirit, and the Spirit against the flesh; and these are contrary to one another, so that you do not do the things that you wish" (Gal. 5:17). The spirit and the flesh are unified in the person of Jesus Christ. Through this unification, the Lord Jesus can unify each of us and make us whole and holy as we were meant to be.

From previous chapters we can see there is an understanding within the early Church, and continuing in the Orthodox Church, regarding sacramental mysteries and how God uses physical material such as water, oil, bread, and wine for His holy purposes. But the Church does not stop there. Paul writes, "I discipline my body and bring *it* into subjection" (1 Cor. 9:27).

The Orthodox Church places an emphasis on disciplining the body and controlling its desires. This emphasis is nearly absent in most forms of Christianity. One of the primary ways to discipline the body, as seen in Scripture, is through fasting. Although fasting can take different forms, in the Orthodox Church, fasting primarily focuses on abstaining from meats and animal products (such as dairy and eggs). The Orthodox sometimes abstain from wine and olive oil in addition to the other foods mentioned. Depending on the strength of the individual, there should also be a change in the amount of food and not simply the types of food consumed.

Orthodox Christians fast from certain foods not because they are bad or unclean, but because controlling the types of food and the amount we eat has a tangible effect on our prayer life and our ability to defeat entrenched sinful habits over time. The goal of fasting is to soften the heart and make each of us a humble temple where the Holy Spirit of God can dwell fully. The effect of fasting is to strengthen the will so that we can make decisions in other areas of our life that go against the sinful inclinations of our bodies. In a way, we might say fasting trains us to overcome temptations. Fasting also has the opposite effect from our typical Thanksgiving Day dinner. Instead of putting us to sleep, fasting allows us to be watchful and prayerful. In the Orthodox Church, the discipline of fasting is so important that it is practiced roughly two hundred days out of the calendar year.

Here are a few examples of fasting in the Holy Bible. In the Old Testament, we have the great example of the people of Nineveh:

Jonah began to enter the city on the first day's walk. Then he cried out and said, "Yet forty days, and Nineveh shall be overthrown!" So the people of Nineveh believed God, proclaimed a fast, and put on sackcloth, from the greatest to the least of them. (Jonah 3:4–5)

In the New Testament we read, "Then Jesus was led up by the Spirit into the wilderness to be tempted by the devil. And when He had fasted forty days and forty nights, afterward He was hungry" (Matt. 4:1–2). This forty-day fast was the preparation the Lord took before beginning his earthly ministry. The Lord also taught:

Moreover, when you fast, do not be like the hypocrites, with a sad countenance. For they disfigure their faces that they may appear to men to be fasting. Assuredly, I say to you, they have their reward. But you, when you fast, anoint your head and wash your face, so that you do not appear to men to be fasting, but to your Father who is in the secret place; and your Father who sees in secret will reward you openly. (Matt. 6:16–18)

Also we see there were cases where healing was not possible without prayers strengthened by fasting:

But Jesus took him by the hand and lifted him up, and he arose. And when He had come into the house, His disciples asked Him privately, "Why could we not cast it out?" So He said to them, "This kind can come out by nothing but prayer and fasting." (Mark 9:27–29)

As they ministered to the Lord and fasted, the Holy Spirit said, "Now separate to Me Barnabas and Saul for the work to which I have called them." Then, having fasted and prayed, and laid hands on them, they sent them away. (Acts 13:2–3)

Here are some examples of this practice in the early Church:

This fasting . . . is very good, provided the commandments of the Lord be observed. (The Shepherd of Hermas, AD 90–140)

Before the baptism, moreover, the one who baptizes and the one being baptized must fast, and any others who can. And you must tell the one being baptized to fast for one or two days beforehand. (The Didache)

As bodily food fattens the body, so fasting strengthens the soul; imparting it an easy flight, it makes it able to ascend on high, to contemplate lofty things and to put the heavenly higher than the pleasant and pleasurable things of life.

The point is not only that we should come to church each day, that we should continually listen to one and the same thing, and that we should fast for the whole Forty Days. No! If we, from continually coming here and listening to the teaching, do not acquire anything and do not derive any good for our soul from the time of the fast all this does not procure for us any benefit.

Fasting is wonderful, because it tramples our sins like a dirty weed, while it cultivates and raises truth like a flower. (Basil the Great)

Fasting is a medicine. But like all medicines, though it be very profitable to the person who knows how to use it, it frequently becomes useless (and even harmful) in the hands of him who is unskillful in its use. (John Chrysostom, On Fasting)

The strictness of the Quadragesima [the forty-day fast undertaken during Lent] mortifies the passions, extinguishes anger and rage, cools and calms every agitation springing up from gluttony. And just as in the summer, when the burning heat of the sun spreads over the earth, the northern wind renders a benefaction to those who are scorched, by dispersing the heat with a tender coolness: so fasting also provides the same, by driving out of bodies the burning which is the result of overeating. (Athanasius)

Do not neglect the Forty Days [Lenten Fast]; it constitutes an imitation of Christ's way of life. (Anthony of Egypt)

The gate is narrow and the way of fasting is hard, that way leading to the life of purity, and there are few to make the journey. . . . Fasting ends lust, roots out bad thoughts, frees one from evil dreams. (John Climacus, The Ladder of Divine Ascent[6])

In addition to the discipline of fasting, the Orthodox also have disciplines such as keeping a rule of prayer (a set of prayers one says daily), making prostrations (bowing or kneeling) while praying, and sometimes even keeping prayer vigils during the night. Each of these disciplines is biblical, and each may be undertaken with the guidance of an experienced spiritual father, because it is important for each of us to have a loving guide who will help us focus on the areas that need strengthening. We should also remember that we don't fast to feel good about ourselves or to become puffed up or prideful. Fasting that leads to pride is of no value at all.

Throughout the Bible we see examples of men and women who wore sackcloth and ashes, who fasted, and who kept vigil and prayed—such as the Lord Jesus Himself. By doing these things, we become like those the Lord speaks of when He says, "The kingdom of heaven suffers violence, and the violent take it by force" (Matt. 11:12). Instead of simply resting on our laurels and imagining ourselves to be righteous before God, we are given a way to do our best to live up to the goal of being "perfect, just as your Father in heaven is perfect" (Matt. 5:48).

For an Orthodox Christian, it is not enough to simply call ourselves "saved." What is important is to "work out your salvation with fear and trembling" (Phil. 2:12). Because we love God, we want to do everything in our power to develop a relationship with Him. This requires controlling the flesh, since "the flesh lusts against the Spirit, and the Spirit against the flesh; and these are contrary to one another, so that you do not do the things that you wish" (Gal. 5:17).

It is up to each of us. Are we content simply knowing about Jesus Christ, the Son of God, or do we really want to know Him? When the physical disciplines are undertaken with guidance and the right attitude, then we are given the great blessing of entering more deeply into the Christian life.

14

The Life of Worship

After hundreds of conversations with folks regarding the subject of church worship, I am struck by how little most people seem to know about the history of the Church. This is not surprising, since people have fallen into the trap of believing that all they need is the Bible. Of course, by now you realize that the Bible without proper interpretation is quite problematic. It can lead to misguided and self-deluded interpretations. This is probably most apparent in the area of worship.

I have met dozens of people who think Jesus Christ was a sort of hippie who did away with the Jewish religion and encouraged His disciples to go out into a field and play a guitar while singing songs about love. These people reject organized religion, imagining the alternative can be called anything but disorganized religion. Some even call themselves "spiritual but not religious"—a phrase that to my knowledge has never been defined coherently.

In other cases, we see that Christians around the world believe in going to church, worshiping, and praising God. They claim to read the Bible, yet the ways in which all these groups come together as church are starkly different. More importantly, they are starkly distinct from anything the Apostles or early Church leaders could have imagined or ever had in mind.

How we worship is central to what we believe, and what we believe is central to how we worship. As we look at the New Testament and the early writings of the Church, we will get a sense of how they viewed worship. That is exactly our goal: to know the mind of the early Church and its understanding of the Scriptures.

The first place to look for a picture of early Christian worship is Acts, since it is a record of the historical development of the life of the Church. In Acts we read, "These all continued with one accord in prayer and supplication, with the women and Mary the mother of Jesus, and with His brothers" (Acts 1:14). We notice their focus was on being together in one accord and in unity while they devoted themselves to prayer. Again we read, "And they continued steadfastly in the apostles' doctrine and fellowship, in the breaking of bread, and in prayers" (Acts 2:42). Again it is worth noting they did not devote themselves to the reading of the New Testament or to individual portions such as the Epistles or Gospels (those did not exist at the time). They devoted themselves to the teachings of the Apostles and to fellowship, to the breaking of bread, and to prayer.

The breaking of bread that is mentioned here is none other than the practice of Holy Communion. As the apostle Paul taught, "For as often as you eat this bread and drink this cup, you proclaim the Lord's death till He comes" (1 Cor. 11:26).

Again in Acts we see the disciples were "continuing daily with one accord in the temple, and breaking bread from house to house" (Acts 2:46). Far from rejecting the temple and Jewish customs of the day, the Christians embraced their faith in the Messiah Jesus as the continuation and perfection of the Jewish religion. They believed in organized religion because they were the fulfillment of an organized religion. We see that they continued the breaking of bread in their homes, as it was unsafe and impractical to do so anywhere else at the time.

In Acts we also read, "Now Peter and John went up together to the temple at the hour of prayer, the *ninth* hour" (Acts 3:1). Again, this is proof that the disciples of the Lord, who knew His teaching and received the gift of the Holy Spirit, still believed in set times of prayer, in organization, and in the temple structure. Also in Acts we read, "Now on the first *day* of the week, when the disciples came together to break bread, Paul, ready to depart the next day, spoke to them and continued his message until midnight" (Acts 20:7). Here we see that this "breaking of bread" is mentioned again as happening on the first day of the week, yet another reference to the practice of Communion on Sunday. We also see the reference to preaching as a necessary activity for the gathering of the Church.

Concerning order and peace in the Church, Paul teaches,

> *How is it then, brethren? Whenever you come together, each of you has a psalm, has a teaching, has a tongue, has a revelation, has an interpretation. Let all things be done for edification. If anyone speaks in a tongue, let there be two or at the most three, each in turn, and let one interpret. But if there is no interpreter, let him keep silent in church, and let him speak to himself and to God. (1 Cor. 14:26–28)*

The verses above make it clear that speaking in tongues, as is so often done in Pentecostal communities, is usually inappropriate. This is true since typically there is no interpreter for the individual who is speaking. More importantly, there is the sense that things are to be done in good order. Order has a place in the life of the Church, whereas spontaneity and chaos masquerading as the work of the Holy Spirit do not.

The early Church believed in the reading of Scriptures. This is highlighted by Paul: "Now when this epistle is read among you, see that it is read also in the church of the Laodiceans, and that you likewise read the *epistle* from Laodicea" (Col. 4:16). This is also seen in 1 Thessalonians: "I charge you by the Lord that this epistle be read to all the holy brethren" (1 Thess. 5:27).

The final aspect of Sunday morning gatherings is mentioned in 1 Corinthians: "Now concerning the collection for the saints, as I have given orders to the churches of Galatia, so you must do also: On the first *day* of the week let each one of you lay something aside, storing up as he may prosper, that there be no collections when I come" (1 Cor. 16:1–2). While the focus of Sunday morning is clearly the breaking of bread, there is still a practical focus on collecting goods and funds for the needs of others.

As we see in the New Testament, the main parts of Sunday morning worship include the reading of Scriptures, preaching, prayer, and the Lord's Supper, as well as the collection for the saints. Let's look at the writings of the early Church for more evidence about church life.

And on the day called Sunday, all who live in cities or in the country gather together to one place, and the memoirs of the Apostles or the writings of the prophets are read, as long as time permits; then, when the reader has ceased, the president [the bishop or presbyter] verbally instructs, and exhorts to the imitation of these good things.

Then we all rise together and pray, and, as we before said, when our prayer is ended, bread and wine and water are brought, and the president in like manner offers prayers and thanksgivings, according to his ability, and the people assent, saying Amen; and there is a distribution to each, and a participation of that over which thanks have been given, and to those who are absent a portion is sent by the deacons. And they who are well to do, and willing, give what each thinks fit; and what is collected is deposited with the president, who succors the orphans and widows and those who, through sickness or any other cause, are in want, and those who are in bonds and the strangers sojourning among us, and in a word takes care of all who are in need.

But Sunday is the day on which we all hold our common assembly, because it is the first day on which God, having wrought a change in the darkness and matter, made the world; and Jesus Christ our Savior on the same day rose from the dead. For He was crucified on the day before that of Saturn [Saturday]; and on the day after that of Saturn, which is the day of the Sun, having appeared to His Apostles and disciples, He taught them these things, which we have submitted to you also for your consideration. (Justin Martyr, comments on weekly worship from First Apology, ch. 67)

Clearly we see the teaching of the New Testament reflected also in the writings of Justin, as he mentions the partaking of Communion, the reading of the Scriptures, prayers, and the collection for the saints.

But every Lord's day do ye gather yourselves together, and break bread, and give thanksgiving after having confessed your transgressions, that your sacrifice may be pure. (The Didache, ch. 14)

Quite the opposite of what one might expect, there is a nearly complete absence on the subject of "praise and worship" music or singing in the New Testament. That is not to say that music and singing are bad, but it is a direct correction of the modern phenomenon of contemporary worship that centers around emotional, almost romantic songs of praise. In fact, in many Protestant (and even quite a few Roman Catholic) churches, the main feature of the church is a stage filled with musical instruments. Music is certainly powerful and can deeply affect people's emotions, but we have to remember that we are not in church on Sunday morning to have short-lived emotional experiences. Instead we are after the spiritual effect that is permanent and life-changing. Music can be used as a kind of drug that gives an emotional high and leaves us wanting more every week.

One of the reasons music plays a featured role on Sunday morning has to do with the mission of evangelism and outreach. As churches look to become "seeker-sensitive," they must adopt the ways of the world in order to be successful according to their definition of success. In order to draw the masses, they must put on a good show, in much the same way people want to be entertained when they stay home and watch television or go out to see a movie.

In the early Church as seen in the New Testament, there is no focus on being seeker-sensitive. Evangelism and outreach are seen as a focus of daily life, but not as a focus when we gather together as believers. This time of gathering together is not meant to evangelize the outside world; it is meant to declare our separation from it and to focus our lives on God the Father and His Son Jesus Christ through the Holy Spirit. Since Sunday is the Lord's Day, it is truly meant to be a day set apart for Him. Far from looking and sounding like the world around us, the church is meant to look and sound like a place distinctly dedicated to the Lord.

Another interesting aspect of most Protestant worship is the amount of prayer (or lack thereof) within a typical service. In my experience visiting many denominations and various services, the practice of communal prayer is nearly absent. Without exaggerating, I have found that very few denominations have communal prayer for more than five or ten minutes on any given Sunday.

Prayer is communication with the Lord, the source of life, love, joy, and peace. If we neglect the source of all these wonderful blessings by refusing to spend quality time seeking His face (Ps. 27:8), then it is no surprise that we are unfulfilled as Christians. While we understand that God is not interested in the length of our prayers, it should still be surprising that we spend so much time on music and singing, which are nearly absent from the New Testament descriptions of Sunday gatherings, while we neglect the areas of Communion and prayer, which are spoken of nearly everywhere.

Whatever the reason may be, it is clear that modern forms of Christianity have lost their way and are frequently looking to reinvent their worship. The hope is that fresh music, flashy PowerPoint presentations, and hip preachers will fill the church, and they often do exactly that. The question is whether all of this can actually fill the void in our hearts and bring us nearer to the Kingdom.

There is another way to worship. In the Orthodox Church, every Sunday morning is a special time when we gather to pray together, led by a presbyter who was rightly appointed by an authentic bishop of the Church. During this time we thank God for His mercies toward us and we eagerly wait upon the coming of the Lord, who teaches us through the words of the epistle, the Gospel reading, and the sermon. Finally, the Lord reveals Himself fully in the bread and wine that are set forth and blessed by the power of the Holy Spirit to become His mystical and spiritual body and blood. Rather than seeking an emotional high, we find ourselves filled through prayer with the Spirit of God. Through communion with the Lord, who is present in the sacred gifts that have been offered, we find ourselves in a powerful union with God Himself. We as the Bride of Christ fully consummate our marriage to the Lord when we come together and worship as one.

Contrary to many assumptions, the Orthodox liturgy is far more biblical than any Christian service in any other denomination. The liturgy is more scriptural in practice but also in actual content. In fact, just a cursory glance at the liturgy of John Chrysostom or Basil the Great reveals that nearly every line is pregnant with biblical imagery and meaning. The Bible becomes our prayer throughout the liturgy and in the various readings that are specific to the day.

The worship of the Church reflects the reality of the Kingdom of God. However, our prayer together as a church is not simply a reflection of the Kingdom. It is an *extension* of the Kingdom. The worship of the Church is a continuation of the worship and glory that are offered before the throne of God eternally. Every Sunday we gather together as the Church, the body of Christ, with all the saints who have gone before us, and together we enter into the presence of God. Our eternal life in paradise will be nothing more or less than this: a perfect and unchanging holy liturgy.

15

The Goal of the Christian Life

The goal of the Christian life, according to the Orthodox understanding, is not to be saved from hell or eternal damnation. Our goal is not simply to get to heaven, either. While those might be good and noble goals, they fall short because they are ultimately rooted in fear. We are told in Proverbs that "the fear of the LORD *is* the beginning of wisdom" (Prov. 9:10). However, for Christians that is only a beginning. Fear has to give way to something greater. As John the Evangelist writes, "Perfect love casts out fear" (1 John 4:18).

The goal of the Christian life is not to be saved *from* something such as punishment or hell fire. Rather, our goal is to be saved *to* someone. In short, the goal is Jesus Christ Himself. As the apostle Paul says, we are to "grow up in all things into Him who is the head—Christ" (Eph. 4:15).

Paul also writes, "We are bound to thank God always for you, brethren, as it is fitting, because your faith grows exceedingly, and the love of every one of you all abounds toward each other" (2 Thess. 1:3). What a great definition of the Christian life! It is one in which our faith isn't stuck in the day that we accepted Christ, but is growing dynamically.

The Christian life features an abundant growth in Christ. It is a life in which our love is increasing, because love is a sign of God in our lives: "God is love, and he who abides in love abides in God, and God in him" (1 John 4:16). It is a life in which we are growing more perfect and are not simply content to stay in a static relationship. A life in which we are dynamically growing in a living relationship with the Father through the Son by the Spirit. A life in which we become "partakers of the divine nature" (2 Pet. 1:4) and share in the glory of Our Lord Jesus Christ (2 Thess. 2:14). That life is not a fantasy or a work of imagination or wishful thinking. Orthodox Christians really believe it is possible, and we have plenty of examples of men, women, and children who have partaken of this life.

God wants to enter into our lives in a tangible, meaningful way. There is no reason for us to speculate and interpret the Bible privately, because we have the blessing of a better way. This way is made open to us by the Church that contends "earnestly for the faith which was once for all delivered to the saints" (Jude 1:3). It is this living faith in the Son of God, Jesus Christ, that was given to the Apostles, handed down throughout the centuries of church life, and has come to us, unbroken and unchanged today. This beautiful, vibrant, and full expression of the faith is available to us now.

As we have seen over and over again, Protestant Christianity has lost some of its way. Rather, it has lost some of The Way. It is certain many of its followers are trying to love Jesus Christ to the best of their ability, but sadly they seem unfulfilled in their spiritual lives. It is not their fault. They have often been misled or simply remained in the dark concerning the many truths we've discussed here.

There is, however, a better way. The early Church was the Church that guarded holy tradition and the Church that gave us the New Testament. It was the Church that offered the medicines of the spiritual life, such as the mysteries of Holy Communion, baptism, chrismation, confession, and the unction of the sick, as well as the apostolic leadership of the bishops, priests, and deacons. It was the Church that honored saints like the Virgin Mary and continues to ask them to pray for us. It was the Church that came together on the first day of each week and partook of the body and blood of Christ. And it is this same Church, the Orthodox Church, that continues unchanged in its practice of the Christian faith today.

If you are convinced of all this, it is time to leave your comfort zone and take a step of faith. This step of faith starts with heartfelt repentance. As Christians we live a life of repentance every day, because "the sacrifice acceptable to God is a broken spirit" and contrite heart (Ps. 51:17 RSV). We need to pray and beseech God to grant us wisdom to understand the many ways we may have "sinned and fallen short of the glory of God." We also must pray that God will reveal His will to us and guide us to the Church that honors the Lord Jesus Christ by steadfastly guarding the faith, doctrine, and worship that were handed to her.

Next, we have to become like the merchant in search of fine pearls. We have to go out and find the hidden Church. This Church that has been hiding in plain sight is the Orthodox Church.

There are many Orthodox churches within the melting pot of America. Finding an authentic Orthodox church puts us in communion with the Apostles and the Church found in the Book of Acts. Finding this Church allows us to receive the many blessings God desires to pour out on us and on all those we encounter.

As a rule of thumb, whenever we encounter a church that uses descriptions such as "genuine" or "true" in their official title, we should be quite cautious. A similar lesson applies to the used car lot with a sign that reads, "Honest Bob's Used Cars." Despite his assurances, Bob may not be so honest! Likewise, there are some who claim to be Orthodox and may not have the pedigree to prove it.

Also remember that learning and reading about the Church is good, but it is certainly not enough. The real learning begins the moment we enter into the life of the Church by attending her services and participating in her reality. The books listed in the appendix will provide helpful resources for those interested in learning more.

Another word of caution is needed here. Some sources of information are easy to find but can nevertheless be harmful to us. As a rule of thumb, avoid Orthodox internet forums if at all possible. As in any public forum, it is difficult to filter out the good information from the bad. This is certainly true when so much of each is present in any given place. These forums have sometimes helped people find fulfillment in their faith, but they are more likely to lead to arguments, polemics, and virtual shouting matches. Such behavior is rooted in pride, which is alien to our Christian faith. Besides, we need to leave the comfort of the internet bubble. God wants us to go out and be part of a real community.

It is good to look for an Orthodox church that is oriented toward welcoming outsiders and seeks to be a home for everyone who enters. It is easier to make friends and feel at home in that type of environment. Try to find a church that prays most of the services in your native tongue so that you can better follow along and enter into the prayerful life of the Church. Be aware that there are wonderful Orthodox churches that maintain the holy faith and doctrine of the Apostles, but simply minister to the needs of their immediate congregations in the language that suits them most. At times that language will be foreign, which makes sense when we remember that the United States is home to many immigrants who were displaced or moved from other countries for one reason or another. Some of these ethnic churches have provided great spiritual comfort even to those who did not understand the language, but for others, attending such a church can be a hindrance to a thriving spiritual life.

Above all else, be patient, humble, and prayerful. Don't lean solely on your own understanding, but seek the wisdom of others, such as Orthodox clergy and Orthodox lay people. Some are very experienced and can guide you in your walk with Christ. There is always more for us to learn and to know, and we have to seek this knowledge with humility. Becoming Orthodox is just a beginning and not a cause for boasting. We never stop learning or growing as Christians, because God is infinite and there is no limit to His love for us.

If we seek, we will find. Don't ever forget that it is God's good pleasure to give us the Kingdom. Why should we settle for churches that offer anything less?

"For I know the plans I have for you," declares the LORD, *"plans to prosper you and not to harm you, plans to give you hope and a future." (Jer. 29:11 NIV)*

Endnotes

1 Philip Schaff and Henry Wace, eds., *Nicene and Post-Nicene Fathers,* Second Series (Peabody, MA: Hendrickson Publishers, 1994), vol. 4, p. 535.

2 NPNF, The Seven Ecumenical Councils, p. 641.

3 NPNF, series 1, vol. 12, pp. 248–262.

4 http://www.newadvent.org/fathers/2811.htm

5 G. E. H. Palmer, Philip Sherrard, and Kallistos Ware, trans., *The Philokalia* (London: Faber and Faber, 1979), vol. 1, p. 82.

6 John Climacus, *The Ladder of Divine Ascent,* trans. Colm Luibheid and Norman Russell (Mahwah, NJ: Paulist Press, 1982), p. 167.

Appendix

RECOMMENDED READING

These books are suggested as a beginning foundation for studies in the early/Orthodox Church.

Bernstein, A. James. *Surprised By Christ: My Journey from Judaism to Orthodox Christianity.* Ancient Faith Publishing, 2008.

Coniaris, Anthony M. *Introducing the Orthodox Church: Its Faith and Life.* Light & Life Publishing, 2007.

Damick, Andrew Stephen. *Orthodoxy and Heterodoxy: Exploring Belief Systems through the Lens of the Ancient Christian Faith.* Ancient Faith Publishing, 2011.

Gillquist, Peter. *Becoming Orthodox: A Journey to the Ancient Christian Faith.* Ancient Faith Publishing, 2009 (1992).

Mathewes-Green, Frederica. *Facing East: A Pilgrim's Journey into the Mysteries of Orthodoxy.* HarperOne, 2006 (1997).

Schmemann, Alexander. *For the Life of the World: Sacraments and Orthodoxy.* St. Vladimir's Seminary Press, 1988.

Ware, Timothy. *The Orthodox Church.* Penguin, 1996 (1963).

Webber, Meletios. *Bread & Water, Wine & Oil: An Orthodox Christian Experience of God.* Ancient Faith Publishing, 2007.

About the Author

The Rev. Fr. James Guirguis is pastor of St. George Orthodox Church in New Hartford, New York. He has given lectures on topics such as early Christian history as well as sickness, suffering, and healing in the Christian tradition. He

 regularly adds material to the *Out of Egypt* weblog. He earned a master's degree from St. Vladimir Orthodox Theological Seminary in 2006. He lives in Utica with his wife Kh. Jennifer and their three daughters. You can contact him through Facebook, Google+ or Twitter. To discuss this book on Twitter, please use the hashtag #ancientpathsbook.

Ancient Faith Publishing hopes you have enjoyed and benefited from this book. The proceeds from the sales of our books only partially cover the costs of operating our nonprofit ministry—which includes both the work of **Ancient Faith Publishing** and the work of **Ancient Faith Radio**. Your financial support makes it possible to continue this ministry both in print and online. Donations are tax-deductible and can be made at **www.ancientfaith.com**.

To view our other publications,
please visit our website: **store.ancientfaith.com**

 **ANCIENT FAITH RADIO**

Bringing you Orthodox Christian music, readings,
prayers, teaching, and podcasts 24 hours a day since 2004 at
ancientfaith.com

CPSIA information can be obtained
at www.ICGtesting.com
Printed in the USA
FSHW011536080719

9 781936 270637